PROFITABLE PUBLISHING TODAY

Start Earning Money as an Author Without Quitting Your Day Job

PROFITABLE PUBLISHING TODAY

Start Earning Money as an Author Without Quitting Your Day Job

Kim Staflund

Polished Publishing Group (PPG)

Profitable Publishing Today: Start Earning Money as an Author Without Quitting Your Day Job

Ebook ISBN: 978-1-988971-42-1
Paperback ISBN: 978-1-988971-43-8
© 2019 by Kim Staflund
Polished Publishing Group (PPG)

Due to the dynamic nature of the Internet, any website addresses mentioned within this book might have been changed or discontinued since its publication.

For writers:

Writing *is* selling in the online world. You are a more precious commodity than you may realize.

CONTENTS

INTRODUCTION

The best way to build a profitable book publishing business is to start writing on part-time basis. Keep the security of your regular full-time job to ensure a steady flow of income while you write. That will ensure your peace of mind along the way. Only when your monthly writing profits match your regular monthly income should you transition to full-time writing. How long this process takes will depend a lot on you. For one writer, the transition took a year; for another, it took five years. In this book, we'll talk about exactly how they, and many others, did it. More importantly, we'll discuss how *you* can accomplish the same.

YOU'RE IN THE DRIVER'S SEAT

Gone are the days when the world's large corporate book publishers set the pace and direction of the entire publishing market. Today, independent authors are now in the driver's seat. The tools are already at your fingertips, and online publishing is the easiest and most affordable way to begin. (And when I say "affordable," I mean almost completely free of charge. Now *that*'s affordable!)

Your only necessary cost will be editing, which will be covered in detail in this book. The fact is, if you want your ebook to be accepted by a discerning population of readers, you'll need to hire a proper editor to help you get things right. I'll show you exactly where and how to find one at a price that suits your budget. In fact, the whole process from start to finish—from outlining a full ebook series to publishing it online—will be covered in this book. By the time you're done reading this, you'll know exactly how to publish a book. You'll know what it takes to successfully sell it, too.

TURN YOUR "SIDE HUSTLE" INTO YOUR *REAL* HUSTLE

Now, back to the two authors I mentioned earlier who started writing part-time and are now earning sizable incomes writing on a full-time basis. I highly recommend you read a transcribed podcast from The Creative Penn blog titled "The Motivation Myth. How High Achievers Really Set Themselves Up to Win with Jeff Haden" in full. During this interview, authors Joanna Penn and Jeff Haden discuss what it takes to make a living from writing. They provide truly helpful and honest advice about how one can transition into being a full-time author. Here's a brief excerpt from that webpage:

> Here's the thing. When people ask me about side hustles and keeping full-time jobs, if you're going to do that, the first thing you have to do is say, "I will be the best at my full-time job of anyone there."
>
> Because typically what happens is your attention starts to drift and you slide in a few things during your regular work time and you're focused on other stuff. And you owe better to your employer, you owe better to yourself and I just think it's a poor way to start.
>
> So, I worked really, really hard at my job which was good but then I worked every night. I worked most weekends. And I just I tried to shorten that cycle because there's a certain amount of time it's going to take on your side hustle for you to build it up to where you can make that your real hustle.
>
> ...I'm lucky enough now that I get to meet some really, really successful people and talk to them about how they got there. None of them ever describe this little lightning bolt moment or "I hacked my way to success" or I found this shortcut that got me there. Every one of them worked harder than everyone else around them

and they had a goal, they figured out how they were going to get there. (Haden, 2018)

Jeff Haden did the work: the "side hustle," as he calls it. He worked harder than anyone else and was able to make writing his full-time job within one year. For Joanna Penn, it took five years to transition into a full-time writer, and it took another four to earn a six-figure income from her new work. Considering she now earns a *multi*-six-figure income doing what she loves, it was worth the upfront hustle.

Will your full-time job ever bring you that scale of success? If not, keep reading. Jeff and Joanna are far from being anomalies. This book covers several more successful writers who are earning as much—and even *more*—from publishing online.

YOUR SIX-WEEK BLUEPRINT TO SUCCESS

This book contains a repeatable, entirely achievable six-week publishing process—a blueprint you can easily follow no matter what type of book series you wish to publish on the United States of America's Amazon, Canada's Kobo, and even Malaysia's E-Sentral ecommerce sites. It also contains case studies of several highly successful independent authors who are already doing these things and earning massive incomes from it. Read this blueprint in full before you publish. Educate yourself about how this process works before you do anything else. Then make a commitment to yourself to follow through with it. Because it works!

WEEK ONE: OUTLINE YOUR ENTIRE BOOK SERIES

I am a perpetual student of this evolving book publishing industry and have been for over 25 years. In 2013 and 2014, I released two books covering today's North American publishing landscape and the types of book publishers that are available (both traditional and contemporary) to help authors with everything from writing and copyright concerns to pricing, distribution, and printing. While those books are still relevant today, they cater to a different demographic than this book does. They detail the full professional process authors must employ if they wish to have their books taken seriously by *all* the players in the book supply chain including the established "bricks and mortar" retailers, publicists, and conventional book reviewers. It is a process that takes a minimum of three months to complete for the smallest of books—even longer for the larger ones—and produces both a physical book (e.g., paperback, hardcover) and an ebook (e.g., .EPUB, .MOBI) that can sell in all the markets worldwide, both online and offline.

But that doesn't work well for everyone, I've learned. More and more, I come across people who want to publish a book for all kinds of different reasons—to promote a business, fulfill a lifelong dream, commemorate a special occasion, et cetera— and they want it done *quickly* (e.g., within four to six weeks), and with a minimal upfront investment. These are the people who would rather utilize online algorithms to grow their readership than spend any amount of money on traditional forms of book promotion. These authors also want full control over their own creative processes and release dates, and they're fine with selling their books online only.

For a long time, I resisted this idea. I held to my belief that it's impossible to produce a quality book within such a short time period, and especially without the support of a full professional publishing team. But then, one evening, while I was researching bestselling strategies for authors, I came across an online *Forbes* article by J. McGregor titled "Amazon Pays $450,000 A Year To This Self-Published Writer." Obviously, that began to shift my thinking. It was an eye-opening piece about a highly successful UK author named Mark Dawson and how he sells massive quantities of books online. Following that, I attended a conference in Columbia, Missouri, where I met a US author named Liz Schulte who also earns a six-figure income selling her books online. A while later, I met an Aussie author named Timothy Ellis through an online Q&A site called Quora, and he willingly shared his personal formula for selling a minimum of 3,000 books online every single month. (You can read more about these authors inside my recent ebook, titled *Diary of an Indie Blogger VOL 2*, that can be downloaded free of charge from your choice of either Amazon, Kobo, or E-Sentral.)

These authors all write fiction. So, I went in search of a non-fiction success story to confirm for myself that this strategy can work for everyone and every type of book—not only fictional novels. With a quick Google search, I easily found a post on The Creative Penn blog about a non-fiction author named Steve Scott. He, too, appears to be using this "rapid release" publishing method in conjunction with various other strategies, some of which will be discussed within this book. (You can read more about Steve's story in the above-mentioned ebook, too.)

The long and the short of it is that each of these authors shares one primary marketing strategy to sell thousands of books every year: multiple, consistent, strategic book launches. The key to keeping their momentum going seems to be releasing a new book online at least every six weeks, if not oftener—a method that clearly agrees with Amazon's cryptic algorithm because it keeps these authors' books at the tops of their respective bestseller lists for longer periods of time. Each new front list title draws in more and more new readers while subsequently increasing sales of their back list titles. In other words, it has a cumulative effect. Book sales appear to multiply month over month if this pace is maintained over the long term.

Independent authors aren't the only ones using "rapid release" publishing to sell more books. Even mainstream thriller author, James Patterson, has jumped on this band wagon with his BookShots line. His reason for publishing books this way may be a bit different than the rest of us, as indicated in *The New York Times* article by Alexandra Alter titled "James Patterson Has a Big Plan for Small Books." After all, he doesn't need the money. But no matter who you are, the results still appear to be the same.

> ...Mr. Patterson is after an even bigger audience. He wants to sell books to people who have abandoned reading for television, video games, movies and social media.

> So how do you sell books to somebody who doesn't normally read?

> Mr. Patterson's plan: make them shorter, cheaper, more plot-driven and more widely available.

> ...He aims to release two to four books a month through Little, Brown, his publisher. All of the titles will be shorter than 150 pages, the length of a novella. (Alter, 2016)

This *truly* is one of the greatest keys to success as an author today: prolific publishing. The single best way to sell books (and build a blog) is to utilize the power of search engines. Ping their algorithms by feeding them new content on a consistent basis. Do this often enough, and they'll reward you by feeding you more traffic. It works the same for an ecommerce site's internal search engines as it does for Google, Baidu, Yahoo, or Bing.

Needless to say, I'm increasingly certain this same strategy can be used to sell *all* types of books—whether fiction, non-fiction, or even poetry. If this intrigues you, then this book will be a great read for you. Obviously, "rapid release" publishing requires a different strategy than traditional publishing does. Some steps will need to be completed in a different order than usual, and others will need to be eliminated altogether to save time. My goal here is to show you a simple strategy that you can easily replicate repeatedly, ebook after ebook. My desire is for you to earn a profit from publishing online.

EARN "PASSIVE INCOME" FROM EBOOKS

When searching for a useful description of passive income for authors, I came across a post by Jeff Rose titled "Passive Income Ideas You Can Start Today" on his Good Financial Cents blog. He lumps together various sources in this list from the more common financial and real estate investments to the newer online marketing options (some of which we'll be discussing in this ebook). Here's what I respect most about Jeff's post: he acknowledges ebooks, blogging, and affiliate marketing as legitimate sources of passive income right alongside high dividend stocks and corporate bonds.

> Let's be honest, if you want passive income for life, you have to get to the point where your assets are earning for you (even while you're sleeping). But first, you'll have to put in one of three things: time, money, work, or all three.
>
> ...There's no magic trick that turns your time directly into money. Instead, you plant seeds so your money will grow, even when you're sleeping or at the park walking your dog. (Rose, 2017)

That's certainly true when it comes to the digital passive income derived from publishing ebooks: there's nothing "passive" about it in the beginning. There is upfront work to be done, and most established authors will tell you it took more than a few books to get the ball rolling.

On the plus side, if you've already written a fair amount in the form of ongoing blog posts or stories that are growing old on one of your hard drives, you're already well ahead in the game. The writing portion of this process usually takes the most time, followed by the illustrations/graphics (if applicable); so, now all you must do is organize that content into a helpful series (or two, or three) and publish each book one after another, six weeks apart or less. Ed Pilkington illustrated this point rather well in his article titled "Amanda Hocking, the writer who made millions by self-publishing online" that was published in *The Guardian* online a few years back.

> In 2009 she went into overdrive. She was frantic to get her first book published by the time she was 26, the age Stephen King was first in print, and time was running out (she's now 27). So while holding down a day job caring for severely disabled people, for which she earned $18,000 a year, she went into a Red Bull-fuelled frenzy of writing at night, starting at 8pm and continuing until dawn. Once she got going, she could write a complete novel in just two or three weeks. By the start of 2010, she had amassed a total of 17 unpublished novels, all gathering digital dust on the desktop of her laptop. (Pilkington, 2012)

The article goes on to describe how, in April of 2010, she published the first of many fictional novels to a few different online platforms and saw sales of roughly nine copies per day as a result. A few weeks later, she published two more novels and saw her monthly sales grow to *hundreds* of books. A few more weeks after that, she published a fourth novel online and was amazed to see her book sales increase into the *thousands* that month! Long story short, she continued publishing every few weeks, and her sales continued to multiply accordingly. The rest is history.

Granted, Amanda's is a rather extreme success story. But the techniques she used to inadvertently become a millionaire—the top two being prolific writing and publishing—are the same techniques many others continue to use with great success to this day. Sometimes, it simply takes a few more books and a bit more time, as was the case for that non-fiction success story, Steve Scott, I mentioned earlier.

> Steve talks about splitting big topics into micro-topics, which stems from his blogging background. His books

are around 15,000 – 25,000 words and delve deep, rather than being the 'be all and end all' megabook which is more like the traditional publishing model.

...The tipping point into a full time income came when Steve fully committed himself to the model of Kindle publishing in Sept 2012, and wrote a book every 3 weeks. The tipping point to the big league earnings was in May 2014 when Habit Stacking took off, and having 40+ books available helped make more income from the back list. Focus on the genre and the niche and write content within that and build up a brand and a series. Be consistent in your writing. Make it a habit. (Penn 1, 2014)

Ryan Biddulph is yet another non-fiction self-publishing machine who uses this "rapid release" formula. In a 2017 guest post he wrote for the PPG Publisher's Blog, he discussed how he had published "126 bite-sized non-fiction ebooks" during the previous three years.

I've had self-publishing success by writing 6,000 to 15,000 word, short and punchy reads on topics I know inside-out. I address specific problems suffered by my blog readers to match my passion and know-how with reader pain points. (Biddulph, 2017)

I think the greatest take-away from these two non-fiction examples is that it's more important to focus on the *quality* of your content than the *quantity* of words you've written. There is no need to add a bunch of unnecessary fluff into a non-fiction ebook just to get it to a certain word count. Basing a book's value and saleability on word count is old-fashioned thinking.

With non-fiction books of any kind, your number one priority is to understand your readers' question/problem, and then answer/resolve it for them as clearly and easily as possible. That's exactly what my purpose is in *this* book. If you're looking for any details that aren't included here, please consult the

Additional Resources section at the back. You'll most certainly find what you're looking for within the full-length book publishing guides and online courses listed there.

In that spirit...

This chapter discussed three impressive, albeit labour-intensive, examples of how indie authors earned passive income from online royalties over time; and their shared "rapid release" strategy is the focus of the first two sections of this book. First, you'll learn how to outline your own ebook series, and then you're going to focus on writing/creating the individual books for that series as quickly as possible. I plan to keep this process clean and simple so you can easily replicate it every six weeks, in your spare time, while still producing an acceptable, saleable ebook each time.

Luckily, there are additional strategies authors can use to supercharge this passive income that require much less time and effort once the ball is rolling. These more passive techniques will be discussed in the final two sections of this ebook.

So, there you have it: real-world, proven strategies that can work for you whether you're writing fiction, non-fiction, or even poetry. You just have to follow a similar "rapid release" formula as these authors did. Let's take a closer look at that formula now.

PICK YOUR PRIMARY TOPIC (SERIES TITLE/SUBTITLE) AND SPLIT INTO SUBTOPICS (INDIVIDUAL EBOOK TITLES)

Jennifer D. Foster, a freelance writer, editor, and content strategist, provided a two-part guest post to the PPG Publisher's Blog titled "The Ins and Outs of Outlines: Plotters Versus Pantsers," originally published in *2016 Novel & Short Story Writer's Market: The Most Trusted Guide to Getting Published.* In it, she discusses both sides to the age-old debate regarding whether or not authors should plan books out ahead of time:

> Behind every successful novel or short story is an outline, right? Maybe. Some authors swear by a detailed plan (they're known as "plotters"), while others, namely those fly-by-the-seat-of-your-pants writers (known as "pantsers" or "SOPs"), despise outlines. New York Times best-selling author Joseph Finder, for example, believes that "writing without an outline is like doing a high-wire act without a net. Some people can do it, but wouldn't you really rather have a net? I would." New York Times best-selling author J.A. Jance, however, says she "met outlining in Mrs. Watkin's sixth-grade geography class in Bisbee, Arizona. I hated outlining then; I hate it now. I do not outline." (Foster, 2017)

Are you a plotter or a pantser by nature? I'll admit I go back and forth between the two, mainly because every one of my 20+ books has come to me a little differently. Sometimes, I'll receive just a simple concept in my mind. I'll write it down, set it aside, and then wait until the next thought comes along to further strengthen that vision. As each new thought arrives, I'll do the same until there's enough substance to begin piecing together the first concrete outline of the whole book and, from there, start filling in the core substance. Other times, I'll receive the end of a book first. The final chapter will already be a crystal-clear vision in and of itself, so then all I'll have to do is go back to the beginning and write to that end … follow the path before me with all its delightful twists and turns. No outline required.

There's no real right or wrong here; so much of this is subjective. But there are a couple of reasons why you may want to outline your entire ebook series ahead of time: one, it will help you (or your hired illustrator, graphic designer, and/or ghostwriter) to ensure all illustrations/graphics and text are created on time for each new ebook in the series; and two, pre-promotion of the entire series can significantly improve your overall sales, so a clear vision of each ebook is crucial right from the start.

For example, here is a graphic I created to pre-promote all four books in one of my earlier ebook series on the PPG Publisher's Blog even as I was still writing the first one:

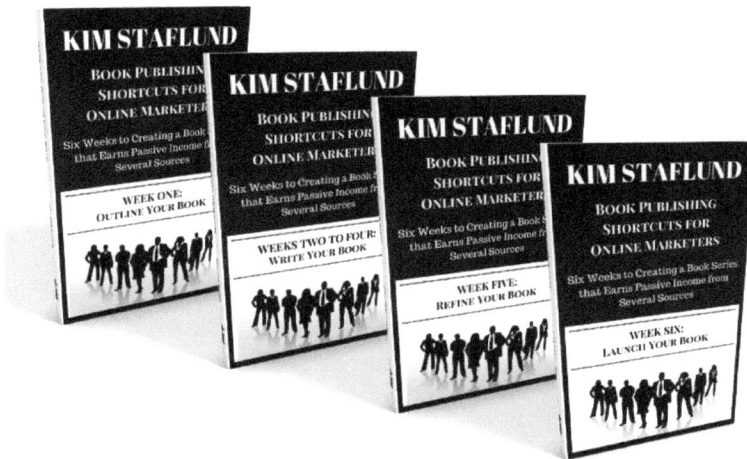

I shared that blog post with an extended list of subscribers and followers via email marketing and social media marketing. I continued doing the same, over and over again, with each new ebook release in order to add fuel to Amazon's algorithm flame.

Which brings me to the whole purpose of this chapter: <u>now</u> is the time to choose your overall topic matter, determine your series title and subtitle based on that topic matter, and further split out your individual ebook titles. You can begin by asking yourself four questions to determine who your target audience is and how you'll best reach them:

1. How old are your readers? What age range?
2. Are they male or female? Or both?
3. What sorts of keywords will these individuals type into a search engine (e.g., Google, Yahoo, Bing, Baidu) to try to find information on this particular topic matter?
4. Which categories will these readers search for your book in when they visit online bookstores such as Amazon, Kobo, and E-Sentral?

Why should you answer these particular four questions for yourself? Well, for starters, knowing the age range and sex of your readers will ensure you design an appropriate book cover that has a strong visual appeal to them. For example, you'll notice the four book covers for that earlier-mentioned ebook series all display the same illustration of male and female business professionals because my target audience for that series is adult online marketers who wish to publish ebooks that generate passive income for them … and hopefully lots of it! I acknowledge that not all online marketers wear business suits and work in a corporate office environment, but the subliminal message of "wealth" and "profit" shines through, which is why I chose that particular image to draw people in.

By contrast, the following ebook cover contains colourful images of children—both boys and girls—reading books while sitting on top of a giant calculator. This imagery ties into the theme of book sales and profits while showing who the primary target market is for the book: school-age children who can read and write, and who have an interest in learning more about the business side of the children's book publishing industry. This is not necessarily an ebook to be read by a ten-year-old alone as much of it will require discussion and further clarification from that child's parents, hence the starburst I added to the front cover that indicates this is "A Family Project for Aspiring Authors." Parents should always be involved in this process along with their children.

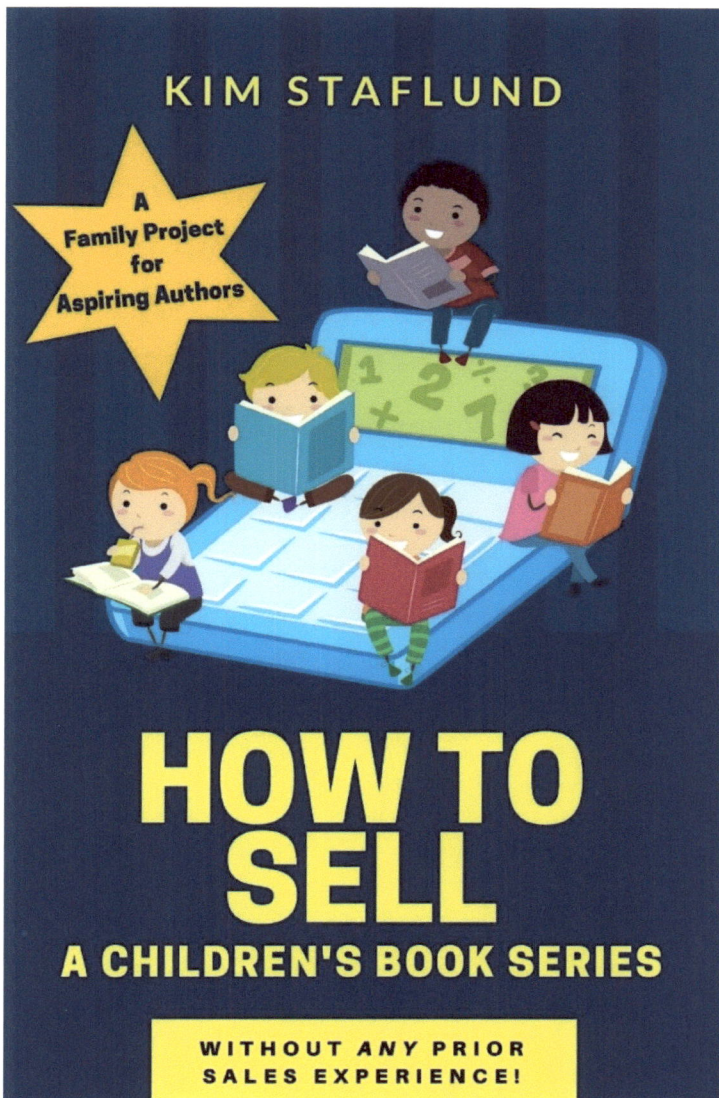

And what if a personal trainer wanted to learn how to create a supplemental book series to promote his or her business? Here's the book cover I designed to appeal to *that* demographic with virtually the same information:

HEALTH & FITNESS AUTHOR

The REAL Secret to Building a Successful Personal Trainer Career

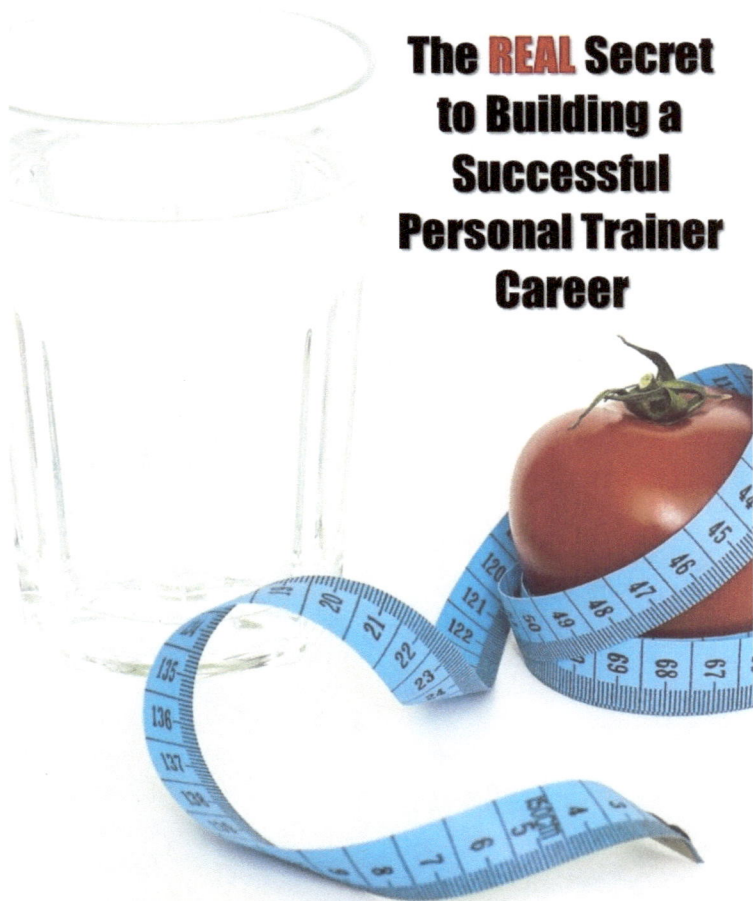

By Kim Staflund

As for this book's cover, I kept things simple. No graphics this time around. Just three concise words to explain the essence of this book: **Profitable Publishing Today**. Sometimes, simple but strong words are all that is needed to get a point across.

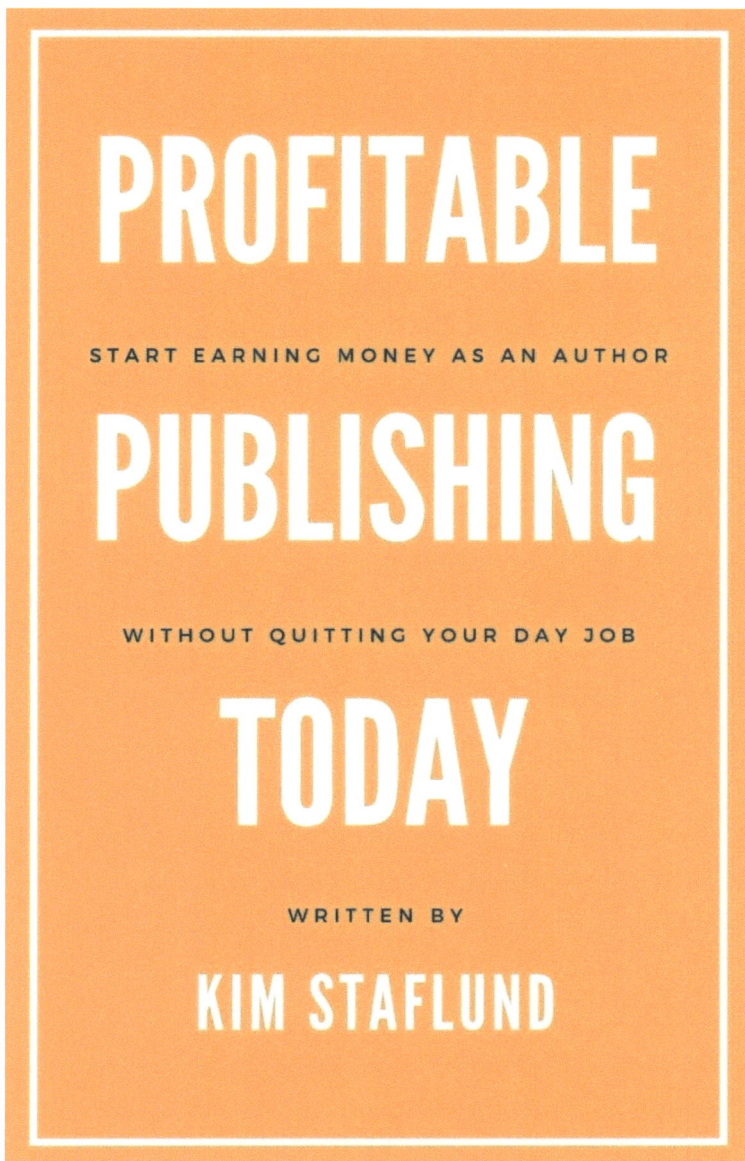

PROFITABLE

START EARNING MONEY AS AN AUTHOR

PUBLISHING

WITHOUT QUITTING YOUR DAY JOB

TODAY

WRITTEN BY

KIM STAFLUND

All that said, an attractive cover is useless if your prospective customers can't find it. That's where keywords and categories come into play. And, for non-fiction books in particular, including all the right keywords in your books' titles and descriptions whenever possible will ensure you come up in all the right online searches. The people who are looking for your particular topic matter will easily be able to find you if you do this right.

WHAT IS A KEYWORD?

In a nutshell, a keyword is a word or phrase that people type into search engines to try to find something they're looking for. When you type a word or two into Google's search box, for example, that will bring up a list of the top related terms people are searching for online, thus giving you a pretty good idea of which variations are going to have the strongest pull for you. Here are some of the main keywords people may type into Google, Amazon, and/or Kobo to search for books such as this one: profit, entrepreneurship, authorship, publishing and books, online marketing, self-help, home based small businesses, business writing, and company histories. "*Company histories*?" you're asking. "Why would anyone ever use *that* keyword to find this book?" This is where things get a little trickier. I chose that particular keyword for a reason specific to Amazon. Allow me to explain.

CHOOSING THE RIGHT KEYWORDS AND CATEGORIES FOR YOUR BOOK

Later in this book, I'll discuss where and how you can easily create your new ebook covers (and even interior graphics) before uploading them to Amazon's Kindle Direct Publishing webpage. For now, all you need to know is that, during this upload process, you'll be choosing two broad categories to place your books into as well as seven keywords that are related to its topic matter. Those keywords are more important to your online success than you may realize, as discussed in a post by Dave Chesson on his Kindlepreneur blog titled "How to Unlock the Secret Kindle Categories."

> Have you ever noticed that when you go to publish your book and select a category on Kindle, certain categories just cannot be found?
>
> After doing hours of research to find that perfect category for your ebook, you discover that you just cannot select it?
>
> As it turns out, Amazon doesn't offer every existing category when you go publish your book. (Chesson, n.d.)

He goes on to explain that your online success is bound to improve if you can get your book listed in additional relevant categories that contain the least amount of competition. The less competition you have, the easier it will be for you to land in the number one spot for that category. The longer you can stay in the number one spot, the more overall exposure you'll have. And the more exposure you have, the higher your sales will be because more people will see and buy your ebook. It all has a cumulative effect.

So, how do you get your book listed in these additional categories? One way is by including the names of those categories within your list of seven keywords. Another way is by incorporating those category names (or portions of them) right into the titles and description details of each ebook in your series—a tactic that works better for non-fiction than fiction, understandably. The crew at Amazon uses these indicators as their cue on where to place your ebook online.

Now back to why I chose "company histories" as one of the keywords for this ebook series. It's because, after a search through my competition, I found that the Amazon subcategory of "Kindle eBooks > Nonfiction > Business & Money > Biography & History > Company Histories" is relevant to my topic matter while being one of the least competitive categories for this type of ebook. Simple as that. As for all the other keywords, I incorporated what I view as the strongest ones into my primary topic matter (series title) while also choosing them as my two main Amazon categories. I used the others for my seven Amazon keywords, to try to unlock additional Kindle categories.

Okay, here's where you stop reading this for a bit. Open up your Internet browser and do a few searches to figure out the top keywords for your chosen ebook series topic. Then go to Amazon's website and explore the various Kindle ebook categories you'd like your series to appear in. Check out your competitor's book covers, categories, titles, and subtitles. For even more information and inspiration, click on their ebooks to look inside at the tables of contents. Based on all that info, play around with the keywords you find to see if/how you may be able to utilize them for your primary topic matter (series title/subtitle) and subtopics (individual ebook titles). Get clear on this very basic outline before moving on to the next chapter of this book.

OUTLINE YOUR CHAPTERS

In the previous chapter, we talked about how useful an outline can be to help guide you to the sorts of information you want to cover in your ebook series and in what order you want to present it. Not only can a well-thought-out outline allow you to pre-promote your series in advance; it can also help you to stay on track with your central purpose, identify any gaps in your reasoning early on, determine which illustrations/graphics you will need to complete ahead of time, and fix any other issues you may come across well before each launch date—all great time-savers for independent authors who wish to write, illustrate, and publish a new book every six weeks. Time is of the essence here, after all.

Now, let's use my earlier ebook series for online marketers as an example since the topic matter is very similar to this book. Below is the initial basic outline I created for that series based on the top keywords I found for that particular topic matter:

PRIMARY TOPIC MATTER (SERIES TITLE AND SUBTITLE)

Book Publishing Shortcuts for Online Marketers:
Six Weeks to Creating a Successful Book Series that Earns Passive Income from Several Sources

SUBTOPICS (INDIVIDUAL EBOOK TITLES)

Week One: Outline Your Book

Weeks Two to Four: Write Your Book

Week Five: Refine Your Book

Week Six: Launch Your Book

By now, you've probably noticed that you can use the exact same process to create an outline for one book as you use for an entire ebook series. To create this single book, I combined those other four mini ebooks together and then repurposed the content to appeal to a slightly different audience (e.g., the primary title is now *Profitable Publishing Today: Start Earning Money as an Author Without Quitting Your Day Job* and the instructions now cater specifically to writers/aspiring authors). Rather than dividing each subtopic into individual ebooks, they became the sections of one book, instead. The rest of the process is the same.

Now, all I have to do is figure out what I want to specifically cover within each of those ebooks/sections. What will the titles of my chapters be? What specific information must I provide to my readers, relative to those chapter titles, that will add the most value? I've kept things *really* simple here for the sake of time, but you may want to add more points and sub-points to your own list. As I said earlier, there's no right or wrong to this. Just keep in mind that you want to complete this project within a six-week period, so it's probably best to keep things as concise as possible. (Unless, of course, you're one of those people who can easily write 1,000+ words per day, every day—then have at it! Write a larger book, so long as it contains *quality* content that your readers will find useful, not just a bunch of fluff.)

Week One: Outline Your Book

- Pick Your Primary Topic (Series Title/Subtitle) and Split into Subtopics (Individual Ebook Titles)
- Outline Your Chapters
- Design and Upload Your Ebook Covers
- Obtain Your ISBNs (Publishing on One Platform Versus Multiple Platforms)

Weeks Two to Four: Write Your Book

- Get Hired as a Ghostwriter
- Write Your Own Book—FAST!
- Why I Still Prefer Microsoft Word to Other Writing Programs (e.g., Scrivener)

- To Index or Not to Index—That is the Question

Week Five: Refine Your Book

- Editing and Proofreading
- Formatting (.MOBI and .EPUB Formats)
- Advice Re: Follow-up Publishing in Other Formats (e.g., Paperback, Audiobook)
- Publish Your Ebook Online

Week Six: Launch Your Book

- Amazon/KDP Marketing (Methodical Launch Timing, Book Descriptions)
- How to Price an Ebook
- Email Marketing
- Affiliate Marketing
- Social Media Marketing

Things will evolve as you go along, and that's fine. You can see that my table of contents is already slightly longer in this book than it was in my original outline, and part of that is because I've included additional front matter and back matter into the book—something you should also do for a more professional result. The initial outline simply helped me to stay on track and on schedule, that's all. It ensured I covered everything that I wanted to cover. (For examples of the types of front matter and back matter you may wish to include in your book, visit this webpage on the PPG Publishers' Blog: https://polishedpublishinggroup.com/the-elements-of-a-physical-book-interior/.)

It's also worth mentioning that doing this full exercise with your first ebook in the series will help to free up time for you down the road. For every other book after that, your full series outline will already be done. And you know what that means, don't you? You'll have freed up an extra week of writing and illustration/graphic design time for each of those ebooks!

Okay, you know what you need to do. Stop reading now. Take the basic outline you created in the last chapter and build on that until you've created your full series outline.

DESIGNING EBOOK COVERS AND INTERIORS

I'll start by saying that, whenever possible, it's always best to hire a professional graphic designer to produce your books for you. There's really no comparison between a book designed by an experienced professional and one created by an amateur using a template. For example, take a look at the books on my personal Amazon page:

https://www.amazon.com/default/e/B0733M2PZV/. The three paperbacks I published in 2013, 2014, and 2015 were all designed by a veteran, and they were later converted to .MOBI and .EPUB formats by yet another expert to ensure each books' interior elements remained properly linked and formatted after the conversion. By contrast, I designed/formatted my own covers and interiors for my online marketers ebook series and this book by myself. They're okay; they're functional. But I can see a notable difference in visual quality between my do-it-yourself books and my other professional-grade books, and I'm sure you can see it, too.

That said, I acknowledge that not everyone has the time or money to pay for these types of services, and others simply prefer a do-it-yourself option. Fair enough. So, in order to intelligently discuss the most effective do-it-yourself options with you, I wanted to experience them first-hand. Here's what I found during this process….

CHOOSING ARTWORK FOR YOUR BOOK

First things first, if you want to include any artwork on your cover, or in your interior, you must ensure you have the legal right to use it. There are three ways you can do this: one, you can use photos, illustrations, or graphics that you have personally created and therefore own the copyright to; two, you can purchase these items from someone else; or three, you can find public domain stock photos that are deemed as "free for commercial use" from whatever design-template program you're using, or from websites such as Pixabay.com, as I did for the mini ebook series mentioned earlier.

It is *crucial* to respect another artist's copyright. If you don't—if you just pull any image file you find off the Internet and use that for your book without first confirming you have the right to use it—you may find yourself involved in an expensive copyright infringement lawsuit down the road. This isn't only about protecting the rights of other artists; it's also about protecting yourself. So, do a little research before you use any images for your ebooks.

EASY AND EFFECTIVE GRAPHIC DESIGN

Luckily, designing an ebook cover is so much simpler than designing a physical paperback cover, as shown in this post from the PPG Publisher's Blog: https://polishedpublishinggroup.com/the-elements-of-a-physical-book-cover/. You only have to worry about the front cover with ebooks.

Amazon's Kindle Direct Publishing platform has a fantastic help section that answers all your "how to" questions regarding creating a new account, cover design, and uploading ebook files to them; so, I recommend you use that resource for every Kindle-specific query you have along the way. Here it is: https://kdp.amazon.com/en_US/help?. That said, I'm not a huge fan of their book cover template—I personally find it quite rigid and limited in design options—so I went with another alternative called Canva: https://www.canva.com/. As it turns out, Canva is not only great for cover design; it's also a great tool for creating picture book interior pages.

I used Canva to create the covers for all the mini ebooks in my series, and I found the templates much more flexible to work with than Amazon's. While both sites are incredibly user-friendly and easy to understand, even for those of us who are not overly tech-savvy, the Canva cover design platform allowed me to more easily manipulate and customize my design. I was able to move things around on each cover until I got them exactly where I wanted them; and that's what makes it such an effective tool for interior pages, too.

EASILY CREATE A PICTURE BOOK FOR CHILDREN OR ADULTS

The interior pages of your ebook are going to be the same dimensions as the cover; so, whether you're creating a picture book for children or adults, all you have to do is use the same Kindle cover template to create every page inside your book as you used to create the front cover. You'll see at the bottom of each template, there is an option to "add a new page." All you must do is click on that option to begin working on the next page using the same template. Add as many pages as you'd like to complete your entire picture book, ensuring they're all in the order you'd like them to appear at publication time.

When it comes time to download the files, there are a couple of options available to you:

1. You can download all the files for your cover and interior pages from Canva as .PNG image files. These image files can then be uploaded into KDP Kids: Kindle Kids' Book Creator (found here: https://www.amazon.com/gp/feature.html?ie=UTF8&docId =1002979921) to create a .MOBI picture book. I recommend this tool because it's free, and it's basically the same process to create a picture book for adults as it is to create one for children. From there, you can convert that .MOBI file into an .EPUB file so it can also be sold on Kobo's ebook platform. (I'll show you how to do that a bit later in this book.)
2. Or, you can simply download them all, in order, as one standard multi-page .PDF file to create an instant .PDF ebook straight from Canva. This format is great for people

to read on desktops, laptops, and iPads, and various other devices; but it can't be read on a Kobo, E-Sentral, or Amazon Kindle ebook reader (which means it can't be uploaded and sold through their websites). Luckily, the KDP Kids tool allows you to upload multi-page .PDF files as well as image files to create your picture book. They've really thought of everything at Kindle, haven't they? I'm more and more impressed with them as time goes on.

Creating and downloading your own cover/interior file(s) on Canva is free of charge, just as it is on Amazon. The only additional cost you might pay on this site will be if you use one of their paid background images/illustrations or their full cover templates. For example, I used a paid background image for my Online Marketers Book Series covers because I didn't want a simple, boring, "flat" black background. I wanted covers with a bit more texture, so I found a background image I liked and paid $10 USD for the right to use it.

CREATING 3D COVER MARKETING IMAGES

When it comes to pre-promoting your book online, it's always nice to create an additional 3D cover image like this one for your blog and/or social media sites:

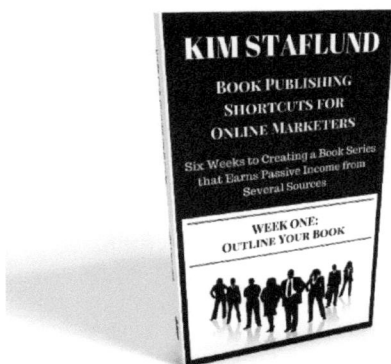

Clearly, it stands out more than the flat images that are created by template builders such as Amazon's and Canva's. I used a free tool called Boxshot Online to create mine: https://boxshot.com/3d-pack/3d-book/.

Again, this is a pretty simple and user-friendly site that can help you to create a 3D image of your book within minutes. All you have to do is upload your front cover from Canva into the spot where it asks for a front cover; and, if you want your 3D image to have a spine just like hardcover/paperback books have, then you will need to create one and upload it into the spot where it asks for a spine. You can leave the back cover portion blank, as no one will see it on your image anyway.

I created pretend spines for my ebooks using Microsoft Word. I simply inserted my Canva cover image onto a blank Word page, and then I created a vertical text box beside it that matched the height dimensions of my cover. I wrote my book title and name into that vertical text box, and then I took a screen shot of the whole image using the "ctrl" and "prt sc" keys on my PC keyboard. From there, I opened up Paint (a standard photo program on all PC computers), and I clicked on the "ctrl" and "v" keys on my keyboard simultaneously to paste that screen shot into the Paint program. From there, I cropped out the spine and saved the new file as a .JPG file separate from the cover image file called "spine file." Easy. Simple.

WEEK ONE: OUTLINE YOUR BOOK

KIM STAFLUND

PPG

The beauty of this is that you'll barely be able to see the spine in your 3D image, so it doesn't have to be a high-resolution image file. You can get away with using a low-resolution screen shot image in this instance.

Once you've uploaded both your original flat front cover and spine images into the Boxshot template, you can play around with various options such as yaw, pitch, contrast, and shadow, and you can even move the book image itself so that less or more of the spine is showing. It's a versatile tool, and it's free of charge to use.

The only portion of this process that will cost you anything is when it comes time to download your 3D images. I paid $10 USD for a 24-hour licence to manipulate and download as many different marketing images as I wanted to for all four of my ebook covers at the same time. "Bada bing, bada boom. Done!"

BOOK COVER UPLOADS FOR PRE-PROMOTION ON KDP SELECT

You don't actually have to complete and upload any of your *interior* ebook files at this point (we'll do that a bit later in this process); however, I recommend you complete and upload ALL your series covers to the Kindle Direct Publishing platform right from the start. There are a couple of reasons why:

1. There's no better way to get yourself to follow through with your own publishing goals than to create deadlines for yourself—for every single one of your books.
2. You can create a *further* sense of urgency for yourself—and anticipation for your readers—by making the first one or two of those ebooks available for pre-order in Kindle stores around the world. (In which case you'll have to upload a fake interior, along with the cover, for the time being.)

One of the reasons you will want to upload all your ebook covers at the same time will be to ensure your metadata (e.g., keywords, categories) is similar for all of them. You can easily achieve this by opening a different browser for each ebook and then cutting and pasting the info from the first one into the others. That's the way I do it. It's one way, not the only way, but just something I want you to think about. Consistency is always key in marketing, but even more so in this case. You want to make sure you're taking full advantage of the Amazon algorithm by ensuring your "rapid release" tactics are hitting at least one or two of the same categories over and over again, six weeks apart, with every one of your books.

Another tool we're going to use here is Kindle's KDP Select marketing program, which will give each individual ebook a little extra "oomph" on Amazon at the time of each release date, so be sure to enroll all your books into this program for at least the first 90 days. As long as an ebook is listed in KDP Select, it cannot appear anywhere else simultaneously (e.g., you cannot also upload an .EPUB to Kobo or E-Sentral while your .MOBI is enrolled in Kindle's KDP Select program). For those of you who plan to publish on Kindle alone, you can keep your ebook(s) listed in the KDP Select program indefinitely and take advantage of the benefits listed here (https://kdp.amazon.com/en_US/help/topic/G200798990) repeatedly, every 90 days. For those of you who plan to publish on multiple platforms, I recommend removing your book from the KDP Select program after the first 90 days, and then begin publishing on other platforms at that time.

We'll discuss the other two publishing platforms, Kobo and E-Sentral, in the next chapter of this book. Amazon is the main focus all the way through only because it is a more detailed and advanced ecommerce site that requires a lot more explanation.

OBTAIN YOUR ISBNS (PUBLISHING ON ONE PLATFORM VERSUS MULTIPLE PLATFORMS)

All books that are being published to sell for a profit must contain an ISBN—with the exception of Amazon Kindle ebooks. Amazon attaches its own unique ASINs to the ebooks uploaded to its site. But every other version of a book must have its own ISBN (i.e., the paperback version will have one, an additional ebook version will have another one, and the hardcover version will have yet a different one).

ASIN stands for Amazon Standard Identification Number. ISBN stands for International Standard Book Number. According to ISBN.org by Bowker,

> The International Standard Book Number (ISBN) is a 13-digit number that uniquely identifies books and book-like products published internationally ... The purpose of the ISBN is to establish and identify one title or edition of a title from one specific publisher and is unique to that edition, allowing for more efficient marketing of products by booksellers, libraries, universities, wholesalers and distributors. (Bowker, 2014)

Each country in this world should have its own national ISBN agency where the authors/publishers from that region can obtain ISBNs for their books. You can find your closest agency via the International ISBN Agency by visiting this link: https://www.isbn-international.org/agencies.

All that said, if you plan to publish your book on Amazon's Kindle Direct Publishing webpage alone, you can skip this chapter altogether. It's irrelevant to you. But if you plan to publish your ebook on additional platforms such as Kobo and E-Sentral, or if you think you may want to produce a paperback or audiobook down the road, then you will need an ISBN for each additional version.

I prefer to publish my ebooks on multiple platforms around the world such as Amazon, Kobo, and E-Sentral, and I recently came across a fantastic post expressing a similar viewpoint that I'd like to share with you. It's titled "How To Self-Publish An Ebook," and it was written by Joanna Penn on The Creative Penn blog.

> ... if you have multiple books in a series and you want to make a living with your writing, then going wide to other platforms is the best idea.
>
> It takes time to build your audience at other stores, and having multiple books in a series is the best way to gain reader loyalty and sales for the long term. Each store has comparative strengths and weaknesses in the different worldwide markets, so building for the future means going wide. (Penn 2, 2017)

Couldn't have said it better myself. And, when it comes to going wide on other platforms, my two favourite choices are Kobo and E-Sentral.

KOBO WRITING LIFE

Kobo's self-publishing platform is known as Kobo Writing Life and can be found here:
https://www.kobo.com/us/en/p/writinglife. Why do I support Kobo? Well, I won't lie to you: part of the reason is that I want to support a company that was founded by a fellow Canadian. But this company also has a user-friendly publishing platform with an increasingly robust worldwide reach that is compatible to Amazon's self-publishing platform. Their whole publishing process is very straightforward and easy to use (as you'll see for yourself once you visit the above link and start publishing there). They have fantastic help resources to guide you along. They pay a slightly better royalty rate than Amazon does (e.g., between 45% and 70% royalties, depending on the list price of your book, versus Amazon's 35% to 70%). As well, I find that it's

a lot easier to make changes/additions to files on the Kobo site than it is on Amazon; Amazon's editing process is more controlled in the sense that they must review and approve all changes you make before reposting a book online for you. I also like that Kobo publishes the same .EPUB ebook format that can also be used on E-Sentral so I only have to make one file (which equates to one ISBN) for both of these ecommerce sites. Amazon uses its own proprietary .MOBI ebook format—another way it tries to control its content and market share. Control is not an entirely bad thing, don't get me wrong. Amazon has a lot of great qualities including *the* single best reporting of any of the ecommerce sites I've used, without question. But Kobo's process just seems a little easier without all those extra controls in place.

E-SENTRAL PUBLISHER'S PANEL

Two years ago, I decided to start publishing on Malaysia's E-Sentral site once I realized that neither Amazon nor Kobo was targeting the southeast Asian marketplace. Having been there myself, this was a market I personally wanted to target and sell to; so, I set up my publishing account with E-Sentral here: https://publisher.e-sentral.com/. This is a relatively new platform that is still growing in terms of the category choices, help resources, and sales reports that are available to its publishers. You're also required to create your own "Preview" file (equivalent to Amazon's "Look Inside" feature) if you wish to allow potential customers to preview a portion of your book before buying it—which has its pros and its cons. Maybe some people prefer to control which content can be previewed; my personal preference is to have someone else create it for me because I already have enough tasks to perform in the publishing and sales of my books without adding yet another one to the list. This publishing platform definitely has a ways to go when compared to Amazon's and Kobo's capabilities, but I'm grateful to be able to reach this marketplace at all.

WEEKS TWO TO FOUR: WRITE YOUR BOOK

In the first section of this book, I highlighted a few different authors who are seeing significant success in terms of the volumes of books they're selling online every single year. These three, in particular, have earned six- or seven-figure annual incomes from their ebook sales and have openly shared their stories in prominent online publications:

- Amanda Hocking was one of the first reported Amazon millionaires who utilized "rapid release" publishing (releasing a new book online at least every six weeks, if not oftener) to self-publish her fictional books after multiple rejections by the traditional trade publishers. Of her success, Ed Pilkington wrote in *The Guardian*:

    > When historians come to write about the digital transformation currently engulfing the book-publishing world, they will almost certainly refer to Amanda Hocking, writer of paranormal fiction who in the past 18 months has emerged from obscurity to bestselling status entirely under her own self-published steam. (Pilkington, 2012)

- Mark Dawson, by contrast, was first trade published. But when he saw how few copies his publisher sold of his fictional novel, he switched to self-publishing and learned how to become an *entrepreneurial* author instead. Of his six-figure success, Jay McGregor wrote in *Forbes*:

    > Dawson's recent success isn't representative of his time in publishing, however. He actually had

a book published by Pan Books called 'The Art of Falling Apart' in 2000, which completely bombed. Not because it was bad - ironically it's now available on Kindle and has 32 five-star reviews out of 39 - but because few people read it or are aware of it. Mark puts the book's failure down to the publisher's inability to promote his work and generate any sort of interest." (McGregor, 2015)

- Steve Scott is a notable non-fiction success story, proving this "rapid release" technique can work for all kinds of books—not only fictional novels. Of his success, Joanna Penn wrote on The Creative Penn blog:

    > If you want a six figure income from your books, it's a good idea to model people who are already making this kind of money. Steve Scott seemed to burst onto the indie non-fiction scene in early 2014, but in fact, he has 42 books and has had an internet business since 2006. (Penn 1, 2014)

These three success stories confirm what I've been writing about and teaching to aspiring and established authors alike for several years now: the most successful authors are the ones who treat book writing, publishing, sales, and marketing as their own businesses. They don't only write; they *sell* their own books. This is true of all self-publishers *and* most trade-published authors, and it's <u>always</u> been that way—contrary to popular belief—which is why people like Mark Dawson are switching over to self-publishing (or supported self-publishing) to produce their books. Why hand the majority of your book's copyright ownership and creative control over to a trade publisher if you're the one who's going to have to sell it, anyway? If my question has raised your eyebrow and you're feeling any sort of resistance to it, then I invite you to read an ebook titled *Why Traditional Bookstores Won't Carry Your Book on Their Shelves … and Why That's Okay* that reveals the many unexpected challenges new authors face when trying to sell their books through traditional channels. It can be downloaded free of charge, anywhere in the world, from your choice of these three ecommerce sites:

Amazon: https://www.amazon.com/dp/B079R41YR7

Kobo: https://www.kobo.com/ca/en/ebook/why-traditional-bookstores-won-t-carry-your-book-on-their-shelves-and-why-that-s-okay

E-Sentral: https://www.e-sentral.com/book/info/201602

Here's the dilemma. Self-publishing still has a bad reputation and is, to this day, referred to as "vanity publishing" by some in the traditional literary community *and* some readers.

> The vanity book publishing model was introduced as an alternative for writers who were tired of waiting around to be accepted by a traditional book publisher and who had instead decided to self-publish their books themselves. As noble as the vanity publishers' intentions might be (to provide another viable alternative to aspiring authors), they are the least respected book publishing alternative of them all within publishing circles (i.e., traditional publishers, reviewers, booksellers, and distributors)—for good reason. These companies are more aptly described as book *printers* than publishers, and they've earned their notoriety by accepting and printing 100 percent of the manuscripts that are submitted to them without much consideration of quality or content—the opposite extreme of trade publishing. A vanity publisher will take what it receives and print it as is—no matter what it looks like. Not only does this reflect poorly on the vanity publisher as a service provider, but it also reflects poorly on the writer. Books that are haphazardly produced in this manner simply cannot compete in the marketplace

against a professional trade publisher's finished product. There is a noticeable difference between the two. (Staflund, 2014)

It takes a team to polish a book to perfection. As the old adage goes, "No man is an island." That's especially true in *this* business. Even Amanda Hocking, who was an avid reader before she ever became a self-published author, could admit that her ebooks were not on par with the quality of traditionally published books. And that really bothered her.

> [A]lthough she has employed [*sic*] own freelance editors and invited her readers to alert her to spelling and grammatical errors, she thinks her ebooks are riddled with mistakes. "It drove me nuts, because I tried really hard to get things right and I just couldn't. It's exhausting, and hard to do. And it starts to wear on you emotionally. I know that sounds weird and whiny, but it's true."
>
> In the end, Hocking became so burned out by the stress of solo publishing that she has turned for help to the same traditional book world that previously rejected her and which she was seen as attacking. For $2.1m, she has signed up with St Martin's Press in the US and Pan Macmillan in the UK to publish her next tranche of books. (Pilkington, 2012)

Notice how traditional publishers finally embraced Amanda once they realized she came intact with her own sales abilities and ready-made platform. Perhaps she was unaware of a *third* option that was available to her at that time: supported self-publishing. Supported self-publishing (also known as hybrid publishing) incorporates the flexibility and copyright retention of vanity publishing with the professional quality of trade publishing. Not surprisingly, it is a business model that is growing in popularity all the time. (Disclosure: supported self-publishing is the business model and publishing process utilized by my own company, Polished Publishing Group, as detailed in both my books from 2013 and 2014.)

The perceived quality of your book is as important to your success as is your ability to sell that book. As we discussed in the first section in this book, one component of quality is the type of content you're providing to your prospective readers. Are you offering something of true value to them—whether it's *entertainment* value in the case of fictional novels or *informational* value in the case of non-fiction books—or is your ebook full of a bunch of useless fluff? Your readers are smart (not to mention inundated by other choices), and they'll be able to see whether or not yours is a quality book with a quick scan of the "Look inside" preview on whichever online publishing platform you've chosen—so you'll want to ensure they see the value straightaway.

In addition to the content you cover in your ebook, how you present that content—the writing itself—is an important component of perceived quality. You can break the writing task into two critical processes: one, the original manuscript that you (or your ghostwriter) produces; and two, the "polished finish" that other professionals such as editors, proofreaders, designers, and indexers add to that original manuscript. In this section, we'll cover how to effectively produce the original manuscript in record speed; and, in the next section of this book, we'll back how important the polishing process is to your overall success—keeping in mind that it is a slightly different process in this "rapid release" publishing world than it is in the traditional publishing world.

GET HIRED AS A GHOSTWRITER

Although some authors both qualify and have the time to write their own books, others might choose to hire a professional ghostwriter to help them create that compelling narrative. Both are acceptable ways to produce a book.

Maybe you're in need of a ghostwriter. Or, if you want to earn a living from writing, perhaps you can contract yourself out as a ghostwriter to other businesspeople in addition to writing your own books. There's some food for thought you can ponder while we discuss how the ghostwriting process typically works....

WHAT IS A GHOSTWRITER?

According to The Free Dictionary by Farlex, a ghostwriter is:

> **n.**
>
> a person who writes a speech, book, article, etc., for another person who is named as or presumed to be the author.
> *[1895–1900, Amer.]*

Ghostwriters (also sometimes referred to as copywriters or content writers) are often hired by business professionals who wish to produce books and various other marketing materials to promote their leaders, products, profession, or educational services. Published books can lend credibility to one's offering if written properly. They can also serve as profitable forms of passive income if published and marketed properly.

WORKING WITH A GHOSTWRITER TO WRITE A BOOK

When hiring a ghostwriter to pen your ebook for you, it is important for authors to remember that ghostwriting is an ongoing, collaborative process. For the sake of efficiency, and to make things run smoothly right from the start, you should have a few things prepared ahead of time, as we've already discussed in section one.

PREPARATION OF CLEAR DEADLINE EXPECTATIONS

Before contacting a ghostwriter with a new book project, it is important to set clear goals regarding when you would like to see your book(s) officially published. Even more crucial, that deadline should be shared with the ghostwriter at the very start of the partnership. This will ensure that both parties are headed in the same direction at the same time. Is this a business history book that must be published and available before a centennial celebration in July? Is this an ebook series that requires several very specific publication dates in order to effectively trigger an algorithm? These are two examples of critical deadlines that must be shared ahead of time. From there, the ghostwriter can backtrack, with the help of the project manager (e.g., the self-publishing author and/or the supported self-publishing company hired by that author), to determine how much time is available for the writing, editing/proofreading, design, and marketing stages of the process to meet that deadline.

PREPARATION OF NOTES

Book publishing is done electronically in this day and age; therefore, it's necessary for all author notes to be prepared in Microsoft Word format ahead of time. If a ghostwriter is supplied with a disorganized set of notes that are scrawled on several different sheets of paper, or provided in several separate email messages, the author's costs will immediately skyrocket because it will take the ghostwriter extra time to organize everything into one file. By contrast, if you supply all your notes to the ghostwriter in one Word document, it will be much easier to follow and begin writing the content within the same file. This is a *huge* time and money saver— which is especially important when it comes to "rapid release" publishing. I'll say it again: time is of the essence here.

Your Word document should be a first draft outline of what you want covered in your series and in what order each ebook should appear—just like the outline we created in section one. From there, the ghostwriter will ask more questions to gain a clearer picture of your vision, and the book will begin to take form.

MENTAL AND EMOTIONAL PREPARATION FOR THE GHOSTWRITING PROCESS

Some authors go into the ghostwriting process with the misconception that, once they've handed their notes to the professional, their job is done and the book will be written. Yes, a ghostwriter can save a lot of time in terms of the writing portion itself. But it is important to understand that you'll be required to answer questions, and may even be asked to review chapters, all along the way. (Much of this depends on the type and size of book being written as well as the ghostwriter's working preferences.)

Authors can also expect to go through a series of emotions during the ghostwriting process. It is natural to feel an initial resistance to each new draft—to feel a bit frustrated if things aren't worded exactly the way you first envisioned. This is a natural reaction, particularly when it comes to personal books like biographies. Recognizing this, I recommend that you read a draft over once, and then put it away for a day or two to give your emotions time to settle. If you do this, it will be easier to read it over again, the next time around, with a more objective mindset. In that objective state, you are then free to change the words you don't like or correct things such as dates, times, and names however you see fit. In my experience, authors tend to make better decisions in the objective state than they do in that initial emotional state.

ANALOGY FOR GHOSTWRITING

A big part of a police officer's job is to write reports—to try to interpret the recollections of various witnesses so they can create the most accurate appraisal of a situation as possible. The biggest challenge in writing this report is that, although each witness saw the same thing, they'll all tend to give the police officer different accounts, mainly because each of them was viewing it from a different vantage point. An officer can only take what he or she is given and translate it as factually as possible. But it's all open to interpretation at the end of the day, isn't it?

Ghostwriters have a similar challenge when it comes to interpreting the notes they receive from authors and trying to turn those words into a readable, marketable book. Sometimes, the ghostwriter might interpret some things a bit differently than the author initially intended. That's okay. It can all be fixed along the way, which is why I say that this is an ongoing, collaborative process.

If you can keep this analogy and these tips in mind throughout the ghostwriting process, then you'll be more patient with it which will make it run much more smoothly for you and your writing partner. In the end, you'll come out of it with an amazing book of which you can both be very proud.

WHERE TO FIND A GHOSTWRITER

In section one of this book, I had written:

> More and more, I come across people who want to publish a book for all kinds of different reasons—to promote a business, fulfill a lifelong dream, commemorate a special occasion, et cetera—and they

want it done *quickly* (e.g., within four to six weeks), and with a minimal upfront investment. These are the people who would rather utilize online algorithms to grow their readership than spend any amount of money on traditional forms of book promotion. (Staflund, 2017)

This is who I wrote this book for. And, presumably, if you wish to spend as little money as possible on book promotion and publishing, then you're also someone who wants to spend as little money as possible on ghostwriting costs. Fair enough. In this case, it's best to hire an enthusiastic freelancer, fresh out of college, who is willing to charge a little less to build up his or her ghostwriting repertoire. (I'll come right out and say this: never expect experienced professionals to give you a cheap price. They've earned their higher rates and charge them for good reasons. You get what you pay for in this world, no matter what it is that you're buying, so keep that in mind.)

A great site to find freelancers of all kinds, with all experience levels, from all over the world, is UpWork.com. You can browse through the ghostwriters already listed there to get a sense of what their hourly or flat fee rates are, or you can post your own job, timeline, and payment expectations to see who replies and take it from there. I've personally used this site as a freelancer (albeit on only one occasion, after which I took on a couple other busy projects that stole all my time); and I can tell you there are many checks and balances in place to ensure the freelancers you're hiring are exactly who they say the are.

Another site you can try is Guru.com. I've never personally used it, but I've heard many good things about it, from people I respect, in terms of the high-quality native English talent you can find there. If you wish to reach a native western-based English audience with your book, and English isn't your first language, then this will be all the more important to you.

For those of you pondering the possibility of contracting yourself out as a ghostwriter for other businesspeople, you can use these two websites to promote your service. If you're new to all this, be sure to start out with lower rates so you can build up your ghostwriting repertoire more quickly and easily.

HIRING WESTERN-BASED ENGLISH TALENT—NOT AS STRAIGHTFORWARD AS YOU MAY THINK

Before we move on, it is important to mention that English is *far* from being a simple, straightforward language—all the more reason for you to hire a professional editor from the particular western-based English region you're trying to emulate in your book. There are many different editorial style guides associated with the English language, depending on which country your editor is representing: United Kingdom, Canada, the United States of America, Australia, New Zealand, and South Africa. We all have different ways of spelling and punctuating the English language, so we each use different editorial style guides when editing books. I'll talk more about this in section three, so make sure to read it because it's an important detail that many authors often overlook. But I wanted to touch on it here to emphasize the importance of it ahead of time, because you'll want to let whichever freelancer you hire know which English style guide he or she should be using when editing your book. (And if the person you're hiring doesn't understand what that means, then find someone else because that person is *not* a proper editor.)

WRITE YOUR OWN BOOK—FAST!

During week one of this six-week process, you mapped out the chapter titles that will appear within each ebook in your series. By doing so, you've already got your roadmap. You know exactly where you're going. That's half the battle won already, believe it or not. Now all you must do is fill in the substance of each chapter over the next three weeks, whether it be writing a text-only non-fiction book or organizing your illustrations/graphics with small bits of text onto each page of a picture book.

So, what's the best way to tackle this? Should you schedule a chunk of time each day and "force" the ebook out, or is it best to work only when the mood hits? These are common questions that many authors face at the prospect of writing a book.

The truth is, *starting* is the easy part. The first few pages and ideas can seem to flow out of your mind faster than your hands can type. This is the most enjoyable stage because it stems from impulsive inspiration, meaning that you're creating only when the mood hits. Unfortunately, if that mood doesn't hit on a regular basis, writer's block can set in.

Creativity is similar to muscularity in that it will begin to atrophy with a lack of regular stimulation. Just as even the finest athletes have those days when they must dig a bit deeper to find the will to carry on, all writers will have the same experience. I've found the following tactics effective in getting myself to keep writing on a consistent basis, and I believe they can work for anyone.

BREAK IT DOWN PER HOUR

You've got three full weeks to complete the first ebook. If you already have a full-time job, that means you've probably only got two or three hours of writing time available per day during the weekdays; but if you're *truly* dedicated to this "rapid release" publishing process, then you'll take at least another six hours per day on the weekends, if not more. That gives you a conservative 81 writing hours in total.

3 hours X 5 days X 3 weeks = 45 weekday hours
6 hours X 2 days X 3 weeks = 36 weekend hours
45 + 36 = 81 writing hours

Commit yourself to this schedule in the very least. Keep this promise to yourself. You'll be amazed by what you can accomplish once you make a firm decision to write for these many hours each week.

Now break it down by hour. How many words can you write in one hour? 100 words per hour will result in an 8,100-word mini ebook at the end of three weeks. 300 words per hour will result in a 24,300-word ebook (around 5,450 words less than this book). 500 words per hour will result in a 40,500-word ebook at the end of three weeks. I don't want you to get too hung up on the word count because, as we discussed earlier, *quality* is more important to your readers than *quantity* is. (My mini ebooks, which are equivalent to one chapter of a standard book, are typically from 5,000 to 8,000 words in length whereas my standard, full-length paperback books are generally 30,000+ words in length.) This simple mathematical exercise was added here only to demonstrate what you *can* accomplish in a short amount of time. When you break it down like this for yourself, it suddenly appears more achievable, doesn't it? And when your goal appears more achievable to you, you'll be more apt to stick with it and see it through to the end.

On the other hand, let's say you're producing a picture book series that contains several illustrations or graphics throughout but very few words. Let's say your goal is to create a 20-page picture book—whether it be a children's book or how-to non-fiction guide for adult do-it-yourselfers—that contains only one or two sentences per page. Well, including the cover, that will be 21 pages to complete—equivalent to one page per day over a three-week period. Totally doable, especially when it's your passion!

SCHEDULE YOUR TIME WISELY

Once you've planned how many hours per day/week you will commit to writing/designing your ebook, you should actually schedule those hours. Mark them in your calendar just as you would any other important appointment such as client meetings, dental/medical visits, or extra curricular activities.

By scheduling regular writing intervals in this way, you will move past that fleeting, impulsive inspiration toward a more lasting, thoughtful inspiration and finish your book in record speed. Sometimes, when settling down to write, you might have no idea what you're going to say—and that's okay. It might take half an hour to get that first awkward sentence out and "unlock the floodgates" of creativity; but most authors are pleasantly surprised with how much they have at the end of each session. It's because the *intention* to create is the very thing that attracts the creation. That's the power of deliberate, thoughtful inspiration.

"Start writing, no matter what. The water does not flow until the faucet is turned on."
~Louis L'Amour

JUST WRITE FOR NOW; DON'T EDIT

Here's another great tip: resist the urge to edit yourself over and over again while you're writing each day. In fact, don't edit yourself at all. Your sole purpose, during these three weeks, is to get your indie ebook written and designed. Period. So, that's all you should be doing. The whole editing process will happen during week five of this six-week journey, so you don't have to worry about it until then. Okay?

Creating a *truly* professional-quality book—including non-fiction how-to books of any kind—is a team effort. The writing portion is typically done within the solitude of one's imagination and writing room. And then there is the "polishing" portion of the process, which is equally important to your success and requires an *outside* team of professionals for best results. So, do your part now, and let them do theirs later. You'll end up with a better book in the end if you do so.

READ REGULARLY

The writers who spend even as little as half an hour per day reading another person's work often find that they are more creative during their own writing sessions. It doesn't even have to be another book, or anything related to your topic matter at all; it can be an online article, magazine, newspaper, or blog. Sometimes, the least likely source can inspire the greatest creativity. The most important point here is to keep yourself open and aware of the infinite pool of ideas all around you. Whatever it takes to get that first sentence out, do it. From there, thoughtful inspiration can—and *will*—take care of the rest. It always does.

ASK YOURSELF THESE SIX QUESTIONS

If you're still having difficulty getting started with a particular chapter after trying all the tips mentioned earlier, then here's another great idea generator. Write these six questions down underneath that chapter title: Who? What? Why? When? Where? How? Now begin answering each of them for yourself in relation to the topic matter at hand. That should get your creative juices flowing if all else has failed on a particular day.

REWARD YOURSELF ALONG THE WAY

It's important to reward yourself throughout this process because writing a book is an accomplishment all in itself. It deserves your recognition!

What sort of reward will provide you with the greatest sense of motivation to continue forward with your goals? A ticket to a sporting event, concert, or movie at the end of one full week of writing? A particular food item after a certain number of words is written? A visit to the local market or leisure centre? Or maybe your idea of a treat is a new pair of shoes once you've completed the whole book?

Whatever it is, treat yourself. Reward yourself along the way. This is a great way to keep yourself on track and motivated because it gives you something extra to look forward to.

ONE PARTICULARLY HELPFUL WRITING TIP

I'll start by including one of my absolutely favourite quotes about writing by Gary Provost from his book titled *100 Ways to Improve Your Writing: Proven Professional Techniques for Writing with Style and Power* (a book I highly recommend you read if you're serious about writing):

> This sentence has five words. Here are five more words. Five-word sentences are fine. But several together become monotonous. Listen to what is happening. The writing is getting boring. The sound of it drones. It's like a stuck record. The ear demands some variety.
>
> Now listen. I vary the sentence length, and I create music. Music. The writing sings. It has a pleasant rhythm, a lilt, a harmony. I use short sentences. And I use sentences of medium length. And sometimes, when I am certain the reader is rested, I will engage him with a sentence of considerable length, a sentence that

burns with energy and builds with all the impetus of a crescendo, the roll of the drums, the crash of the cymbals—sounds that say listen to this, it is important. (Provost, 1985)

It's beautiful, isn't it? It's like music, as he says. This is the kind of writing that will keep an audience engaged. It not only sings to them; but, with the right combination of vivid adjectives and visceral verbs, it can create such authentic, powerful imagery inside their minds that it keeps them turning the pages for more. That's really what you're after whether you're writing fiction *or* non-fiction. Don't you think? Try to make your book as "musical" as possible for best results. Motivate your readers to stay with you by relaying stories, examples, and/or descriptions throughout your book that will appeal to their *emotions* just as music does, and you'll surely keep them engaged.

I hope the stories I've shared about authentic author successes are music to your ears, in a non-fiction sort of way, and motivate you to follow this plan from start to finish. That's their purpose. These stories are the living, breathing proof that this plan *can* work for you just as it has worked for others. But it can only work if you follow it with consistency and purpose.

WHY I STILL PREFER MICROSOFT WORD TO OTHER WRITING PROGRAMS (E.G., SCRIVENER)

Depending on the type of ebook you're creating (e.g., text-only fiction or non-fiction books, poetry with artwork, picture books for adults or children), you're going to be adding different components to its interior as described in detail in this post (https://polishedpublishinggroup.com/the-elements-of-a-physical-book-interior/) on the PPG Publisher's Blog, and in summary here:

> The **front matter** of a book might contain some or all of the following components:
>
> • Primary title page
>
> • Secondary title page
>
> • Copyright page
>
> • Quote page
>
> • Dedication page
>
> • Acknowledgments page
>
> • Foreword
>
> • Preface
>
> • Table of contents
>
> The **body** of a book usually contains at least the following two components:
>
> • Title pages
>
> • Sections or chapters
>
> The **back matter** of a book might contain some or all of the following components:

- Appendix

- Bibliography (a.k.a. citations)

- Glossary

- Index

- Promotional Content

- Author Biography

Go to your local bookstore one day this week. Browse the section related to your book's topic matter to see how the hardcover and paperback interiors are formatted there. Then look at some of the ebooks you find online. That will help you decide how you would like to design your own book's interior.

I often read other authors' blog posts and articles so I can keep up with the latest trends in book writing, sales, and marketing. Lately, I've been hearing a lot of buzz about a program called Scrivener. Many consider it to be *the* greatest tool for today's writers—as opposed to simply *a* great tool—so, I wanted to learn more. I watched some very well-produced video tutorials describing this program's capabilities to see whether I should purchase it for myself. In in the end, I decided to stick with Microsoft Word. If you're writing non-fiction in particular, then I recommend you do the same when it comes to your ebook. Here's why.

From what I gather, Scrivener has features that enable you to add annotations, comments, and footnotes to your book, and you can even export your file to .PDF, Word, and two of the most widely known/used ebook formats: Kindle's .MOBI format and Kobo's .EPUB format. This is wonderful—particularly the ebook conversion functionality. That alone may make me buy the program down the road. Scrivener appears to be a great organizational tool for the writers who are producing long, arduous projects requiring them to manage a lot of different elements; however, it has limitations when it comes to writing (and *editing*) some of the above-mentioned front matter and back matter in one's book. These limitations are the reason why I prefer to stick with Microsoft Word as my primary writing tool, particularly for non-fiction books.

What I find most useful about Microsoft Word is that it's used by virtually everyone all over the world, and the company has an amazing network of tutorials and help available to all these users whether they are using a Mac or a PC. That's really important when a document is being shared among multiple people such as authors, ghostwriters, editors, designers, indexers, and ebook converters. Pretty much everyone is using Word. Everyone everywhere. For the authors who are using Scrivener to write their books, they typically have to export their files to Word format in order to send it to someone else to view, anyway; so, why not just complete the whole project in Word to begin with? That was the question I kept asking myself while watching those video tutorials. (If you want to challenge me on this, go for it. I welcome it because I'm always open to learning better ways of doing things. Write me a comment in the online reviews section of this book. I promise I'll read it and take it into consideration. I am a life-long learner.)

Here is something else to consider: Word already has many well-developed, built-in capabilities that will automatically create things such as a table of contents, citations with an associated bibliography, and an index *for* you as you write your book. All you have to do is insert those elements into your document right at the start, and then you can easily update them with a click of the mouse all along the way, at any time you choose.

That said, the standardized formats that Word uses for bibliographies and indexes usually need to be tweaked by editors and indexers, depending on the editorial style guide that is being used for the book. This is something we'll discuss a bit more within the next section of this book, along with the promised discussion about western-based English language editing. I'll even show you how to convert your Word files to .EPUB and .MOBI ebook formats once the editor has finished polishing your Word file.

We'll also discuss one more reason why I prefer Microsoft Word over other writing programs: the editing tool, also sometimes referred to as "track changes." What an amazing tool this is! Basically, it allows you to compare your original text against any changes/recommendations an editor has made to that text and then accept or decline them as you see fit. This is a truly important tool for all independent authors who want maintained control over their creativity.

TO INDEX OR NOT TO INDEX—THAT IS THE QUESTION

I hire a professional editor, graphic designer, proofreader, and indexer to help me produce every single one of my standard, full-length, non-fiction paperback books. Then I hire an additional ebook conversion specialist to turn those book files into .EPUBs and .MOBIs for me. There are several sets of eyes on every single one of my standard books to ensure 99% accuracy and the most polished result possible. (I'll never guarantee 100% to anyone because we're all human. Even *The New York Times* has typos in it. But 99% accuracy *is* possible with the right team of professionals in place.)

Indexes are a very important component of non-fiction paperback/hardcover books. Some people think they're irrelevant to ebooks, but I would tend to disagree. I'll tell you why—but, first, you need to understand exactly what an index is in order to appreciate just how important it is to non-fiction readers.

To fully appreciate the difference between the computer-generated indexes that programs like Microsoft Word produce for you versus a customized index created by a professional indexer, I invite you to read a guest post by Tia Leschke on the PPG Publisher's Blog titled *The Index as a Roadmap*. To sum up what she's saying, an alphabetized index is used to help readers pinpoint the exact pages where they can find an important name, place, or subject throughout the book. It provides a much more precise, defined search result than the table of contents at the front does; and it can make or break the sale of a non-fiction paperback in a traditional bookstore. Why? Because many readers will only buy a non-fiction book after they've scoured the index to see whether specific information they're looking for is contained within.

With ebooks, usually the index isn't even shown as part of the "Look inside" feature on an online store. So, the lack thereof wouldn't prevent someone from buying an ebook. That said, readers who have bought your non-fiction ebook in the past may want to review it again in the future. And, perhaps, there is a certain name, phrase, or event they want to reference again but they can't quite recall the word(s) they're looking for. This is the perfect example of a time when they will refer to the index to trigger their memory. Then they can do a keyword search (or simply click on the index link) to find it within the ebook again.

An index is one of those little extras that add professionalism to a book, just like all the other front and back matter components mentioned earlier. I personally recommend you add one to your non-fiction ebook—particularly if you also plan to convert that ebook into a paperback later on—so that it already has all the proper elements in place for each version.

As you can see, we have much more to discuss in the next section of this book. Let's go there now.

WEEK FIVE: REFINE YOUR BOOK

A lot of people misunderstand the very different roles of editors and proofreaders in the book publishing process; so, before moving into the bulk of this section, I want to provide an explanation of each role. I also want to talk more about what I mentioned in the last section—all the different western-based English editorial style guides there are to choose from and why you might use one over another for your particular ebook project. I'll start with this excerpt from my full-length publishing guide, from 2014, titled *How to Publish a Bestselling Book ... and Sell it WORLDWIDE Based on Value, Not Price!* that describes the traditional paperback polishing process:

> Where a copy editor's job is to review and improve an author's raw manuscript, and the graphic designer's job is to arrange that raw edited text into a professional and appealing layout, a professional proofreader provides yet another pair of eyes to ensure that all the components fit together properly and the book is ready for public viewing and printing. The proofreader's job is to complete the following nine-point check:
>
> Interior Check
>
> • The front matter (such as the table of contents) is accurate and correct.
> • The back matter (such as the index) is accurate and correct.
> • Headers and footers are accurate and correct.
> • Bad breaks, widows, and orphans are eliminated.
> • Text is kerned to flow smoothly throughout.

- Margins and trim size all measure properly.
- Spelling and punctuation is correct.

Cover Check

- Spacing, bleeds, and trim size all measure properly.
- Spelling and punctuation is correct.

As shown in the above list, a professional proofreader is someone who is knowledgeable and experienced with both basic language editing (spelling and punctuation) as well as the technical aspects of book design (kerning, bleeds, trim size, et cetera). If the proofreader finds any issues in the layout, he or she will indicate these and send them back to the designer to make the corrections. Once these corrections are completed, a second hard copy (physical proof) of the book is printed and sent to the self-publishing author for one last overview before the final approval and sign-off of the book. (Staflund, 2014)

Now, this is where things get tricky. While it's in your best interest to have as many different pairs of eyes as possible on your book, to catch as many of those last-minute typos as possible before publication, this practice also comes with its challenges. This is because you can give the same work to three different editors, and each one of them will copy edit it differently from the others. Every single time. Without exception. And then your proofreader will make even *more* changes that will seem to contradict these editors' recommendations ... *unless* you specify which editorial style guide they should all be using right from the very start. In other words, there's no "one right way" to do this, which can be very confusing/frustrating for us authors at times.

Granted, not all authors will find this frustrating. Some of it depends on your personality type: Are You a Red, Blue, Yellow, or Green Personality Type?

(https://medium.com/@LoveFromEC/are-you-a-red-blue-yellow-or-green-personality-type-by-colette-morris-d10ad7d4e27a) Green and yellow personalities tend to be a bit more laid back with this type of stuff because they don't require formal structure and consistency in their working lives; they strive to nurture and preserve their personal relationships with other people above all else. Me, on the other hand … I'm a red personality whose business motto is "Be quick. Be concise. Be gone." I want to get things done. Now. And when I'm frustrated, confused, or overwhelmed by what I consider to be a bunch of unnecessary details that are wasting my time, I turn blue in nature—but not the effective side of a blue personality—and tend to suffer from "paralysis by analysis" as a result. I get stuck in all those details and can't easily get myself out of them. So, you can imagine what inconsistency and a lack of structure does to a mind like mine. *Oy vey!*

I've learned this the hard way over the years (not only with myself but with other red authors who have published through my company). It led to the following discussion with a couple of my company's freelance editors which, in turn, led to an effective solution that will surely help colourful authors everywhere. My company now creates a customized editorial style sheet for every single one of our authors, to ensure consistency in editing for each of their books going forward. The styles are driven, first and foremost, by the author's preference (if any) as to which primary guide he or she wishes to use (e.g., *The Oxford Style Manual* for British authors, *The Chicago Manual of Style* for American authors, a special blend of the two for Canadian authors, et cetera). From there, the customized editorial style sheet is created by the primary editor, and everyone else follows that editor's lead—for every single book published by that author going forward.

Which primary editorial style guide should you start with? If you don't know for sure, that's a discussion to have with your editor ahead of time. It may depend on which country your target market of readers is located in. It may also depend on the type of book being written. Different guides are used for different reasons, and your editor will know best which one(s) to use as the foundation for your personalized style sheet if you don't.

I highly recommend these three things to every single aspiring and established author who is reading this book:

1. Always have your book professionally copy edited in the very least.
2. Whenever possible, use the same editor for every single edition of your book.
3. Have that editor create a customized editorial style sheet that he or she will follow for every single one of your books going forward, and that any other editors/proofreaders can also follow in the future.

By doing so, you'll achieve a more polished result come publication time. You'll also achieve consistency in the editing style of *all* your books going forward.

The editing/proofreading process discussed in this book will be slightly different from the traditional process mentioned in my earlier books. This is because time is of the essence in this "rapid release" publishing world. Your editor will have only one week to complete his or her work for you.

Let's take a "quick, concise, and condensed" look at that process now (music to my red ears)….

EDITING AND PROOFREADING

In section two of this book, I recommended that you just stick to writing your ebook during weeks two through four and save the copy editing to week five. Now's your chance to thoroughly look things over. Take a day to read your manuscript from cover to cover. Do your own quick copy edit now and tweak any last-minute issues with things such as your table of contents, bibliography, index (if applicable) and spelling before sending it off to an editor to have it professionally polished.

LAST-MINUTE TWEAKS

As we discussed in the last section, Microsoft Word already has many well-developed, built-in capabilities that will automatically create things such as a table of contents, citations and bibliography, and an index for authors who are writing non-fiction. You just have to insert the templates for these features into your document ahead of time and then refresh them every once in a while, to ensure the page numbers and links are all updated throughout. The best instructions on how to do so are included in Microsoft's very own Office Help & Training website here: https://support.office.com/en-us/.

Once you've done this, it's time to hand things over to your editor. Your editor will now look at everything through the lens of the editorial style guide you've mutually decided to use as the foundation for your ebook series, and the polishing process will begin.

WHERE TO FIND AN EDITOR

As mentioned in the last section of this book, two great sites to find freelancers of all kinds, with all experience levels, from all over the world, are UpWork.com and Guru.com. When looking for a professional editor, you not only want to discuss which style guide you'll be using for your book; you also want to discuss the level of editing you want done to your work.

Yes, not only are there different editorial style guides to choose from. There are also different levels of editing that can be completed on your manuscript depending on the type of publisher you're dealing with, the type of project you're working on, and the budget you have allotted to the publication of your ebook.

TRADITIONAL FORMS OF EDITING

Traditional literary publishers put each and every manuscript through a very thorough and professional process of substantive/stylistic editing, copy editing, and then proofreading to ensure a polished and saleable result. There are several pairs of eyes on every raw manuscript and galley proof all the way through the process to ensure that 99 percent of every last error is caught and corrected before it goes to print. Here's a brief description of what each of those editing processes looks like.

COPY EDITING

A copy editor will thoroughly review your manuscript in Microsoft Word format and correct any issues with spelling, grammar, and punctuation throughout. He or she will also make helpful suggestions regarding word choice and sentence structure, using the western-based English style guide of your choice (i.e., Canadian, British, American, Australian, South African, et cetera). The edited version will be returned to you for final approval before moving onto the next publishing stage.

STYLISTIC EDITING

Sometimes, you want a little more than a copy edit. A stylistic edit will cover all the points of a copy edit, plus it will eliminate jargon and redundancies, clarify meaning, and ensure that the writing matches the intended audience. Stylistic edits should also be completed using the western-based English style guide of your choice (i.e., Canadian, British, American, Australian, South African, et cetera). The edited version will be returned to you for final approval before moving onto the next publishing stage.

SUBSTANTIVE (STRUCTURAL) EDITING

Do you want the help of a professional editor to improve the overall structure of your manuscript? A substantive edit will cover all the points of a stylistic edit, plus it will clarify and reorganize your story for you. These changes are typically negotiated with you all along the way and are, again, completed using the western-based English style guide of your choice (i.e., Canadian, British, American, Australian, South African, et cetera). The edited version will be returned to you for final approval before moving onto the next publishing stage.

Obviously, there is no time for the full traditional editing process in this "rapid release" publishing world. You're going to want to stick with a copy edit alone, so this should be communicated ahead of time to whichever freelance editor you hire. Copy editing takes the least amount of time, compared with the other levels of editing, and it also costs the least amount of money. Since you're looking to save costs in editing, then the same advice applies here as what I said about ghostwriters. It's best to hire an enthusiastic freelancer, fresh out of college, who is willing to charge a little less to build up his or her editing repertoire. Never expect experienced professionals to give you a cheap price. They've earned their higher rates and charge them for good reasons. You get what you pay for in this world, no matter what it is that you're buying.

USING MICROSOFT'S "TRACK CHANGES" FEATURE TO COMPLETE AN EDIT

Your copy-edited manuscript will be returned to you in Microsoft Word format with the "track changes" feature turned on. Using this tool, as described on the Microsoft Office Help & Training website (https://support.office.com/en-us/), you'll now be able to pull up the reviewing toolbar which contains all the user-friendly tools you'll require to review and address the editor's suggestions one by one. You can accept and decline each change as you see fit; and, I'm willing to bet you'll accept 95% or higher. You'll be amazed by what an editor's eyes will find that you weren't able to see after viewing your own manuscript several times over. I'm certain you'll be grateful that you invested in this type of support.

Once you're finished reviewing everything, you'll want to go back through your document one more time to make sure all the changes were either accepted or rejected. When you click on the forward or backward arrow now, you should get the message, "Word found no tracked changes." That's how you'll know the manuscript is clean and ready for a final proofread.

A CONTEMPORARY FORM OF PROOFREADING

Now it's time for proofreading. You can easily spare one or two days for this, following the copy editing process, and still meet the six-week publication deadline for your book. This is because the two steps that follow proofreading—ebook conversion and the actual online publishing process—are both fairly quick actions that shouldn't take you more than one day combined to complete. Remember, we already did much of this publishing and marketing set-up (book cover design) when we created our outline at the very start.

In the traditional publishing world, your book is sent to a professional proofreader for another once-over before publication. In the "rapid release" publishing world, you can proofread it yourself, one last time, to save time and money; or, you can do what many of today's entrepreneurial authors are doing to ensure that polished result we're all after. Authors such as Mark Dawson and Don Massenzio are combining proofreading together with a form of market research in order to sell more books: they're using their top fans as beta readers. In his blog entry titled "The Importance of an Editor and Beta Readers for Independent Authors," Don Massenzio explains how using your own loyal readers as focus groups can improve the quality and enjoyability of your books for everyone:

> Beta readers are early previewers of your book that read through it after the editing process is complete. They look for story element inconsistencies and other elements of your book from the perspective as [sic] a fan and a reader. It's a good idea to pick a couple of readers that are big fans of your writing, but are not afraid to give suggestions. This process is like having a focus group or preview audience for your product that gives their opinion to you on a small scale before you release it to the relentless general public. Beta readers will spot things in your book that you and your editor missed such as inconsistencies in character traits, likability of your characters, and other intangibles. This is especially importance [sic] if your characters span more than one book in a series. You don't want to publish a book in a series that has continuity issues with previous books. (Massenzio, 2015)

I'll admit I have two concerns regarding this form of proofreading: one, while it may help with things like character trait consistency, it may well cause further editorial *inconsistency* unless all these beta readers are aware of (and know how to use) your customized editorial style sheet; and two, it sounds a bit time-consuming to me. It's challenging enough to get *any* book completed and published in six weeks with only a ghostwriter/author, editor, and designer involved never mind if a group of fans are also added into the mix.

That said, I mentioned Mark Dawson in the first section of this book because he is a highly successful and business savvy author that was mentioned in *Forbes* as earning $450,000 per year selling his books online. Mark not only writes and publishes several books per year, but he also uses beta readers to improve each books' saleability come publication time. So, this technique is definitely worth consideration. It is a new take on proofreading that may well be the wave of the future.

> One of the practices that many Indie authors have implemented is an advance or beta team of readers who serve the author in a few very important ways in exchange for a free, advanced copy of the book. #1 - These readers help tighten up plot holes, errors, and oversights through feedback as they read the book. #2 - They provide reviews on Amazon and other retailers once they [*sic*] book is live on their platforms. #3 - They also can be a great source of encouragement and affirmation for the author. Mark's beta reader team was fairly large (over 700 people) and they were very active in this most recent launch. (Dawson, 2016)

It's up to you: hire a professional proofreader; proofread it yourself; or, use beta readers to proofread your book. At the end of the day, the path you choose will depend on your budget and personal preference. But I *do* recommend a final proofread of some kind, however you get it done. It will polish your book even further than a copy edit does which should positively impact your sales in the long run.

SELF-EDITING TOOLS FOR INDEPENDENT AUTHORS (AS RECOMMENDED BY PROFESSIONAL EDITORS)

Self-editing will never completely replace the value of a professional *human* editor for your books. But these self-editing tools can certainly help.

I recently came across an article written by Amanda Shofner, and further edited by the TWL Team, on The Write Life website. I take the advice regarding these editing tools seriously because of who is giving this advice:

> During self-edits on my latest manuscript, I experimented with six editing tools, both free and paid, to determine which could be most beneficial to The Write Life's audience. Besides being an author, I'm an editor, so I also weighed each tool against what I'd look for when editing.

> ...An automatic editing tool doesn't replace a human editor. Because language rules and elements of a good story can be so flexible, human eyes will always be superior to the rigidity of automatic tools. (Shofner, 2019)

According to Amanda and the TWL team, each self-editing tool has its strengths and its weaknesses. None can be used for everything.

SELF-EDITING TOOLS FOR SPELLING AND GRAMMAR

Not surprisingly, Grammarly is first on the list of self-editing tools. We've all been inundated with Grammarly advertising lately, so it's a popular brand. You can download and start using a free version of this tool to help with self-editing your blog entries. Unfortunately, you can expect to be continually bombarded with even more ads if you do so. They won't stop until you upgrade to a paid version. At the end of the day, The

Write Life team recommends Grammarly for basic grammar and spell checking. I personally think you can get this same value from Microsoft Word ... and without all the advertising interruptions.

The next recommended tool is called ProWritingAid. This also has a free version available (for a limited time) so you can try it out before buying it. It takes things a step further by helping you catch over-used words and repeated phrases.

After the Deadline is next in line. This grammar tool is completely free of charge, so it's perfect for bloggers on a budget. That said, the team at TWL cautions "you get what you pay for" here. They recommend Grammarly above it.

SELF-EDITING TOOLS FOR ANALYZING READABILITY

The Write Life team recommends AutoCrit as a great tool for fiction writers. They also speak highly about this paid tool's ability to analyze and correct one's common writing issues. More sophisticated than any of the earlier-mentioned tools, it can help in the developmental editing stage of a manuscript.

Next up is the Hemingway App. This free online app needs to be used in conjunction with other grammar and spell-checking apps. Why? Because it doesn't check those things. What it does is analyze your writing to improve its readability.

Last, but not least, there's WordRake. This one is a fairly pricey add-in for Microsoft Word or Outlook, and with good reason. You get what you pay for in life. And here's what these editors have to say about this tool: "WordRake is a great tool for the copyediting stage. Verbose writers, authors wanting to cut down on editing costs or editors looking to speed up their editing process will most benefit from WordRake." It sure sounds worth the investment!

FORMATTING (.MOBI AND .EPUB FORMATS)

Up to now, I've always hired outside help to design my paperback covers and interiors for me, and then I've hired additional outside help to convert those files into proper .MOBI and .EPUB ebook files for me. That still remains my preference to this day. I would have preferred to hire outside help for this book, too; but, in the spirit of time management and efficiency, which is what I'm teaching in this book, I learned how to do these things for myself. Are my results as professional as they would have been with that experienced outside help? Honestly, I don't think so. But I think this book is functional and saleable. We'll see. (You'll let me know, won't you? Please do. Write a review to let me know your thoughts.)

In section two of this book, I mentioned a popular writing program called Scrivener that has ebook conversion functionality, allowing you to export your written document to both .MOBI and .EPUB formats fairly quickly and easily direct from your writing tool. (Calling Bill Gates … if only Microsoft Word could do the same, my writing life would be complete!) I could have purchased Scrivener and learned how to convert my ebooks using their tool; but I chose two free programs that I found online, instead, since our goal here is to not only save time but also money.

Just because I've chosen these particular programs doesn't mean they're the only programs you should consider. I invite anyone reading this book, who knows of a better tool than what I'm suggesting here, to please write your advice/opinion/experience in your book review and attach it to this book online. Let's help each other here. Although I have over 25 years' experience in this industry, I'm still learning every day, and I remain open to learning more.

On that note, here are the two free tools I've been using to convert my Microsoft Word files to ebooks: Calibre Ebook Management (https://calibre-ebook.com/) and Online-

Convert.com (https://www.online-convert.com/). Why two different tools? Allow me to explain.

I first decided to go with Calibre after reading a blog post by Jane Friedman titled "How to Turn a Microsoft Word Document Into an Ebook (EPUB)" found here: https://janefriedman.com/word-epub/. My main reason was because Calibre is a free ebook conversion tool that someone like me, with no prior experience converting files of this nature, finds the most user-friendly of all the tools I've come across during this journey. Secondly, when I first downloaded it, it appeared I would be able to just as easily convert my Word files to .MOBI ebooks (the file type used by Amazon) in addition to .EPUB ebooks (the file type used by Kobo, E-Sentral and many other ecommerce sites). I thought, "Great! One easy fix for both file types!" Think again.

While I was easily able to convert my Word document into both ebook file types, a scan of those converted files showed me that certain things (e.g., my indexes, a couple of my headings) were a bit garbled; so, I had to slightly edit the html code within the converted files, using Calibre's edit tool, to get things back to how I wanted them. Unfortunately, Calibre only allows you to edit .EPUB files.

Online-Convert.com to the rescue! Luckily, I was able to find this free conversion tool that allowed me to upload my edited .EPUB files directly to their site and quickly convert them to properly edited .MOBI files. No additional formatting or editing required! Within one minute, the site downloaded the .MOBI directly to my hard drive for me. A quick scan of it showed that all was well—no garbled content. That's it, that's all. Done!

And I have some more great news for you about Online-Convert.com. You can take the .MOBI picture book file you created in KDP Kids (as discussed in section one of this book) and convert that into an .EPUB using this online tool. That .EPUB can then be uploaded to Kobo Books for sale.

ADVICE RE: FOLLOW-UP PUBLISHING IN OTHER FORMATS (E.G., PAPERBACK, AUDIOBOOK)

Presumably, the majority of people reading this are more interested in producing ebooks than any other format. Many of today's independent authors choose to create ebooks first and then convert them down the road, if the need arises, using free do-it-yourself tools such as CreateSpace for paperbacks or Audacity for audiobooks. If only it were that simple.

WHY STRAIGHT EBOOK-TO-PAPERBACK FILE CONVERSION JUST DOESN'T WORK

Anyone looking to convert an ebook to a paperback is doing so because they wish to expand their horizons by selling to an offline audience in addition to their online audience. I can tell you, firsthand, that there is much more to consider regarding traditional offline marketing than you may think there is. Everyone trying to sell any type of book needs to familiarize themselves with *all* the different players in the book supply chain, how these players can help you to sell more books, and what these players expect to see in your books before they'll even pay attention to you, never mind help you.

For starters, traditional paperback books are formatted quite differently from ebooks. Where an ebook generally only has a front cover, a paperback book has a back cover, spine, and front cover combined: https://polishedpublishinggroup.com/the-elements-of-a-physical-book-cover/. Even the layout of a paperback's interior is more involved than the layout of an ebook interior: https://polishedpublishinggroup.com/the-elements-of-a-physical-book-interior/. Ask anyone who has ever tried to convert his or her ebook directly into a paperback book using a free online template, and that author will tell you the interior formatting was all screwed up and the cover looked barren and incomplete. To put it bluntly, the book looked like garbage.

You would be better off to start out with a paperback book saved in Word.doc format and convert *that* file to an ebook using the instructions in this book. It will convert better for you. Or, better yet, simply create two different files at two different times—start fresh with both formats. Otherwise, you're in for a formatting nightmare that may well turn you off independent book publishing for life. To help out the indie authors who wish to produce both formats, I recently published a book titled *How to Design a Paperback Book Then Convert it to Ebook Format* that can be downloaded anywhere in the world, from your choice of these three ecommerce sites:

Amazon (paperback and both fixed-layout and reflowable ebook versions are available):
https://www.amazon.com/dp/B07BVJ84JV
Kobo (both fixed-layout and reflowable ebook versions are available): https://www.kobo.com/ca/en/ebook/how-to-design-a-paperback-book-then-convert-it-to-ebook-format
E-Sentral (both fixed-layout and reflowable ebook versions are available): https://www.e-sentral.com/book/info/203256

SELLING PHYSICAL BOOKS TO AN OFFLINE MARKET

Selling physical books to an offline market requires a slightly different strategy than selling ebooks online. Where your digital selling approach revolves around utilizing keywords, algorithms, and various search engine optimization (SEO) techniques to improve your ebook's visibility, your offline strategy will include the use of "bricks and mortar" booksellers, reviewers, and publicists (a.k.a. real people) to bring more exposure to your book. Publicity is GOLD to any author—no matter what type of book you've published, no matter where or how you're trying to sell that book. A positive review from a reputable book reviewer can generate an amazing amount of publicity for you ... but they have certain expectations of physical books.

The professional reviewers want to see a properly (professionally) designed book, and they won't pay attention to anything else much less review it for you. They expect to see all the proper cover design and interior components before they'll ever take it seriously. For one example, they will want to see a proper index at the back of a non-fiction book—a section most non-fiction ebooks are lacking, which is one of the reasons why I've talked about the importance of adding an index into your ebook earlier in this series (just in case you decide to create a paperback version of it down the road).

If you start with the ebook first, and then try to convert it to a paperback after the fact, it will be missing many of these necessary components. The result is that the book won't be taken seriously by reputable industry reviewers and publicists— the ones who can generate that golden publicity for you in the offline marketplace.

WHO OWNS THE ARTWORK?

Here's one more important consideration when it comes to paperbacks....

Before using *any* company's online platform to convert and sell your book as a paperback, first make sure you understand any possible copyright implications that may result. What exactly do I mean? Allow me to explain by sharing this excerpt from my full-length publishing guide, from 2014, titled *How to Publish a Bestselling Book ... and Sell it WORLDWIDE Based on Value, Not Price!*:

> In addition to my book publishing background, I also worked in the world of print advertising sales for many years. What these two industries have in common is that each business (be it a newspaper, magazine,

telephone directory, or book publisher) creates artwork for its respective clients as part of its overall service offering.

A company's artwork policy can vary: some companies believe that once you've paid for and published a creative work, the copyright belongs to you and you can reproduce it at your discretion as part of your own marketing campaign. Other companies believe any artwork that they have created for you belongs to them and can only be reused with their permission at an additional charge. (Staflund, 2014)

In other words, when you're using another company's online template to create or convert your book cover and interior files, you will want to make sure you understand whether they expect exclusivity in return for their services. By "exclusivity," I mean do they expect you to sell that version of your book on their platform alone? Do they expect you to use their printing services alone? I'm not saying these terms are right or wrong. I simply want you to understand the possible implication of such terms, particularly when it comes to paperback books.

Ecommerce retailers, such as Amazon, utilize print-on-demand (POD) technology to sell physical books online. In other words, they won't print and store any physical copies of your paperback book in a large warehouse anywhere. Instead, they'll store only the digital cover and interior files that you've uploaded to their site; and they will print, bind, and ship only as many copies as someone buys from them at any given time. If someone goes to their site to buy ten copies of your book, then ten copies will be printed, bound, and shipped to that buyer. If another person buys only one, they'll print, bind, and ship only one—hence the term "print on demand."

This technology is a wonderful thing in terms of saving authors the upfront expense of printing and storing hundreds or thousands of books. And the print quality tends to be reasonable, too. But what if your goal, in creating a paperback version of your book, is to print hundreds of copies and sell them direct at trade shows or some other venue? Now you may run into trouble because POD technology is only cost-effective for printing from one to 99 books. If you want to print from 100 to 999 books, you'll want to use a digital printer for the best possible cost per unit. And for 1,000+ books, you'll want to use an offset printer for the best possible cost per unit. I recently published another helpful ebook, specifically about printing, titled *3 Book Printing Tips for Indie Authors: Consider This Before Printing Any Books*. It can be downloaded anywhere in the world, from your choice of these three ecommerce sites:

Amazon (available in both ebook and paperback formats): https://www.amazon.com/dp/B07CNRDQN9
Kobo: https://www.kobo.com/ca/en/ebook/3-book-printing-tips-for-indie-authors
E-Sentral: https://www.e-sentral.com/book/info/203350

The moral of this printing story is that, if you've had your physical book created through a company that wants exclusivity of your sales and/or printing, and if that company utilizes POD technology alone to sell paperbacks/hardcovers online, you may be limited to printing and selling only a few books at a time through their site; or, you may end up paying astronomical prices to print 100 or more books through their POD presses.

Find out what their terms are *before* you use their services to convert your ebook to paperback format. Make your decision, from there, as to whether or not it's worth it. It may be. But, then again, it may not be. You may decide to hire a professional graphic designer to help you produce the physical version of your book and then find a local printer to print them for you.

AUDIOBOOKS: YOUR OWN VOICE OR SOMEONE ELSE'S?

I mentioned Audacity, earlier, as a free tool you can use to convert your ebook to audio by recording yourself reading your book. According to a blog post titled "Should You Turn Your Book Into an Audiobook on Audible?" by Matt Stone, Audacity is a decent tool for do-it-yourselfers who want to produce an audiobook as cost effectively as possible.

> It's some trouble no doubt to do it yourself. But like anything else, once it's done and behind you, it doesn't seem like such a big deal. A decent audiobook can be created in about 40 hours (based on a 50,000 word book, much less for a shorter book), and really only requires a decent USB microphone (usually $50-100) and a free program called Audacity. That may not produce rock-your-socks-off audio quality, but it's certainly enough to give your readers a positive listening experience, and enough to get you in the audiobook game. That is, of course, if you have a decent-sounding voice. (Stone, 2017)

Your alternative is to hire voice-over talent—which can be found from the long list of freelancers on Fiverr.com—to produce a professional, musically-scored audiobook for you. The site displays a long list of both male and female talent to choose from, at all different price points; and, much like Upwork (one of the sites I recommended earlier for finding freelance ghostwriters and editors), Fiverr has controls in place to ensure you're happy with the result before your funds are released to the freelancer as final payment.

Whichever way you choose to convert your ebook to an audiobook is fine. It's all up to you and your budget, of course. Once you've done it, you can upload the audio files to Audible, Amazon, *and* iTunes in one fell swoop via ACX.com, and begin selling your audiobook online. Or you can save the audio files on your own website, or on a stack of CDs, for direct distribution to your targeted clientele.

PUBLISH YOUR EBOOK ONLINE

In order to meet your deadline of publishing an ebook within six weeks, you're going to want to upload the final files to Amazon's Kindle Direct Publishing platform near the end of week five, or in the early-to-mid part of week six at the very latest. This is because, once you upload everything and press that publish button at the very end, Amazon—and Kobo, and E-Sentral—will need some processing time in the background before your ebook will officially show up online. What they're doing, during that processing time, is setting up the "Look Inside" feature for your ebook and choosing all the appropriate categories based on the recommendations you provided to them on the Kindle Ebook Details page. You want to make sure you give them ample time to complete their task, and you also want to give yourself some extra time to review what they've published in case it needs any further tweaking. I've found that, sometimes, the "Look Inside" file displays rather sloppily at first, and I have to send them a quick email to get them to fix it. To their credit, they're pretty decent about correcting these types of things quickly.

Step two and page two of this publishing process is where your ebook's final .MOBI interior will be uploaded. You'll recall that your final cover file was already completed and uploaded along with a fake interior file during week one of this process. This was done so you could begin pre-promoting the entire ebook series on your blog or website, via social media, and on Amazon's pre-order list. The only thing to do now is upload the final interior file and launch the Kindle ebook previewer to make sure it's all fine. Then click on "save and continue" at the bottom and move to the pricing page.

There are different schools of thought on how to price an ebook that I'm going to address in much detail in the final section of this ebook. For now, I recommend you choose your pricing and royalty rate based on your own best guess of what your readers would pay for a book like yours. Compare your book to similar books within the same genre—but not only on Amazon. Check out Kobo ebooks. Check out E-Sentral ebooks. And check out paperback and hardcover books in the traditional "bricks and mortar" bookstores to see how the traditional publishers are pricing similar books. Choose a price and trust your own gut on this, then press publish. You can always change it later on, if you decide you want a higher or lower price.

WEEK SIX: LAUNCH YOUR BOOK

In section one of this book, you learned:

- how to outline your own ebook series in full;
- how and where to design your ebook covers free of charge—including both flat and 3D marketing images—so you can begin pre-promoting your entire series online well in advance of publication;
- how to upload those covers to Amazon's Kindle Direct Publishing (KDP Select) platform, to take advantage of pre-orders;
- how to easily create a picture book for children or adults;
- how to choose the most effective keywords and categories for your particular topic matter;
- where to obtain ISBNs, depending on where you live in the world, for any additional versions or formats of your book(s) that you may wish to create down the road;
- and *why* you may wish to publish on additional platforms such as Kobo and E-Sentral.

In section two, you learned about:

- where and how to hire a ghostwriter, at an affordable price, to write your ebook series for you (or how to promote your own ghostwriting services to other businesspeople);
- how to write/design each ebook by yourself as quickly and easily as possible;
- two popular writing tools—Scrivener and Microsoft Word—and my opinion on the pros and cons of each in this "rapid release" publishing world;

- and the benefit of indexing non-fiction ebooks just as traditional publishers do with non-fiction paperbacks and hardcovers.

In section three, you learned about:

- the *true* value of hiring an editor to help you polish your book, and where to find a good one at an affordable price;
- an innovative way that some of today's most successful independent authors are combining market research and proofreading together to improve their book sales at launch time;
- a couple of easy do-it-yourself tools that can be used to convert your edited manuscript into either an .EPUB (the ebook format used by Kobo and E-Sentral) or a .MOBI (the ebook format used by Amazon);
- and some careful considerations and helpful tips regarding converting those ebooks into paperbacks and/or audiobooks down the road.

In this final section, we're going to discuss the marketing aspect of digital book publishing in more detail—specific to the "rapid release" publishing world. We'll talk about how to price an ebook and how some of today's most successful independent authors are using email marketing, affiliate marketing, and social media marketing to super-charge their launch day sales. Let's get started now.

AMAZON/KDP MARKETING (METHODICAL LAUNCH TIMING, BOOK DESCRIPTIONS)

In researching the success stories discussed throughout this book, and really drilling down on what sorts of actions these authors are taking to bring about their phenomenal sales, I've found two commonalities between them all: one, they're utilizing "rapid release" publishing (releasing a new book online at least every six weeks, if not oftener); and two; they're interacting directly and regularly with their readers in meaningful ways, through various means (e.g., email marketing, social media marketing). These techniques not only strengthen their readers' loyalty and probability of buying more books in the future; the whole process also appears to effectively ping Amazon's algorithm.

What does it mean to effectively "ping" an algorithm, you're asking? It means to trigger Amazon's ecommerce site in a way that increases the exposure of an item, bringing it to the attention of more and more potential buyers. Here is an excerpt from an online article titled "Keys to Understanding Amazon's Algorithms" by Penny Sansevieri that explains this concept well:

> Did you know that much like Google, Amazon is its own search engine? The Amazon algorithm, though not publicized directly by Amazon, is something that can really help to boost the exposure for your book once you understand it.
>
> When you're looking for better ranking with Google, most search engine optimization (SEO) experts will tell you to look at keywords and tags as well as on-and off-page SEO factors. The same is true for Amazon though there is one additional component Google does not have: categories. For this piece, we'll dig into two main elements of Amazon ranking: keywords and categories,

both of which can greatly affect your page/book exposure. (Sansevieri, 2013)

Sansevieri's advice, specific to choosing the right categories for your books, resonates well with Dave Chesson's advice that I shared with you in section one of this book.

> For most marketing people, the word "obscure" sends shivers down our spine. Generally obscure is synonymous with failure or, you know, something that's impossible to find.

> But on Amazon this is a very different ballgame. The best categories are the ones that are slightly obscure if not totally so. (Sansevieri, 2013)

She goes on to explain how placing your book in a relevant, but relatively vacant, category will increase your chances of landing in the number one position within that category. From there, magic can happen that boosts your book to new heights:

> If your book hits #1 in that category the Amazon algorithm can kick in and you might see your book paired with other titles, or on a recommendation list with other high-profile books. (Sansevieri, 2013)

Penny is correct when she says the choice of "obscure categories" conflicts with the traditional approach to marketing books. In reading her article even further, it becomes clear that writing an effective book description is *also* very different in the online world than how traditional (trade) publishers and marketers have done it in the past. For example, when their editors come across a word or phrase that is repeated ad nauseam within any text, their instinct is to find alternatives to break up that repetition so the text is more pleasing to read. But online? The more repetition—particular when it comes to your top key words—the better! Also, in the traditional world, you never want your descriptions to be too wordy. Traditional advice has always been to keep one's back cover copy as short and concise as possible, partially because of how small the canvas is; you don't want it to appear too crowded. But things like this work quite differently in the online world:

> While it may seem like you want something short and sweet (so many people don't like long book descriptions, right?) this is where the algorithm either kicks in, or doesn't, based on the word count.
>
> You must have at least 500 words in your book description. Why? Because too little content won't register well (if at all) with Amazon and Google won't pick it up, either...
>
> Another note about your primary keyword: it should appear 2 to 5 times for every 100 words in your book description. So, no keyword stuffing, certainly, but using the keywords in a way that will help ping Amazon's algorithm and also get you some attention in Google, as well. (Sansevieri, 2013)

Like I said in section three of this book, selling physical books in an offline marketplace is different from selling digital books in an online marketplace. In the traditional offline world, you're appealing to *people* such as booksellers, reviewers, and publicists to help you sell more books; but, in the online world, you're working with intangible algorithms and computerized search engine optimization (SEO) processes to increase your exposure. To be successful in the digital world, you must switch your thinking from traditional methods and look at things in a new way.

For example, take a look at the book descriptions for my two mini ebook series: note the repeated use of the phrase "T-shaped marketing" in the *T-Shaped Marketing* book description (https://www.amazon.com/gp/bookseries/B0757319PV/); and note the repeated use of the keyword "online marketer" within each *Book Publishing Shortcuts for Online Marketers* book description (https://www.amazon.com/gp/bookseries/B07573YTB2/). The primary keyword is included in the main title of each series and also scattered throughout the book description at least once or twice per paragraph to ping Amazon's (and hopefully also Google's) algorithm.

Now, compare those to the book descriptions of my full-length paperback books (which are simply duplicates of each book's back cover copy): *How to Publish a Book in Canada*, *How to Publish a Bestselling Book*, and *Successful Selling Tips for Introverted Authors*. Totally different ballgame. Totally different marketing approach that appeals more to an offline crowd than the online world.

ENSURE YOUR BLOG ENTRIES ARE SEO-FRIENDLY TO DRIVE EVEN MORE TRAFFIC TO YOUR BOOKS

Yesterday's advice regarding writing the most SEO-friendly blog posts was similar to Sansevieri's advice regarding writing an effective book description. Make sure your post is genuinely helpful and contains at least 500 words. Within those 500 words, your main keyword should be repeated at least 10 times. By doing that, search engines like Google should be able to easily find and index the blog entry based on that keyword.

Today's advice is a little bit different. According to _SEO 2019_ author Adam Clarke and Yoast: SEO for Everyone, writing each blog post with an SEO-friendly Flesch Reading Ease Score (FRES) is crucial to your SEO success.

> Google have been outspoken about readability as an important consideration for webmasters. Google's former head of web spam, Matt Cutts, publicly stated that poorly researched and misspelled content will rank poorly, and clarity should be your focus. And by readability, this means not just avoiding spelling mistakes, but making your content readable for the widest possible audience, with simple language and sentence structures.
>
> ...The Searchmetrics rankings report discovered sites appearing in the top 10 showed an average Flesch reading score of 76.00—content that is fairly easy to read for 13-15 year old students and up.
>
> ...By encouraging search results to have content readable to a wide audience, Google maximise their advertising revenues. If Google were to encourage complicated results that mostly appeal to a smaller demographic, such as post-graduates, it would

lower Google's general appeal and their market
share. (Clarke, 2019)

This statement makes me smile not only because it encourages
editing, but also because it matches my own business
philosophies that drive how I write my blog entries and books,
and how I run my book publishing company. I've always
maintained that when people are unable to explain their topic
matter to others in layman's terms with ease, they're either
hiding something or they don't fully understand it themselves.
I'd rather be clear and helpful. I was glad to learn the team at
Google sees it the same way. Clearly, I'm in good company in
this regard.

WHY I NOW USE THE FREE YOAST SEO WORDPRESS PLUG-IN

In a nutshell, the free Yoast SEO WordPress plug-in helps me to
write blog posts that Google will approve and index. That's why
I use it. Because Google is the greatest link between me and my
desired reader base.

As I begin writing each blog post, the Yoast plug-in continually
gives me little notices. It lets me know whether my content is
SEO-friendly in various ways. It tells me if my FRES is within the
acceptable 60.0 to 70.0 readability range. If not, it will show me
which sentences need to be adjusted to improve that score.

YOUR BLOG POSTS CAN BE 300+ WORDS LONG

So long as your writing style matches Google's desired FRES
score, your post can be 300+ words long. Yoast also has a
different way of viewing keywords. Rather than repeating your
top keyword at least twice within every 100 words, Yoast wants
to see it right upfront. If you include that keyword in your slug
(the URL for the blog entry), at least one or more of your
headings, *and* within your first paragraph, Yoast will usually give
you a good SEO score. It's also great to attach the keyword to

an image on your blog post, too. That way, Google will certainly understand which keyword you want the post indexed under. Make sense?

There are additional things you can do to improve your blog post's SEO. Including internal links to past blog posts and external links to other relevant information will also help. The more posts you write that Yoast awards a good readability and SEO score to, the higher up your blog will land in Google's search engine ranking under several different keywords.

I talk more about effective blogging, among other proven online tactics, inside the following trilogy. I highly recommend you download these ebooks to complement this one:

The Author's Holy Trinity of Profit

The Author's Money Tree
How to Grow a Bountiful Readership Organically
Kim Staflund

The Author's Gold Rush
How to Harvest a Bountiful Crop Repeatedly
Kim Staflund

The Author's Magic Key
How to Stay on Track and Keep the Faith
Kim Staflund

ACTION
Whether you self-publish or sign with a traditional publisher, you'll need a fan base (a.k.a. platform) of willing buyers to sell your books to.

Here's your action plan to build that fan base—a plan that some of today's top authors are using to earn six-figure incomes.

THOUGHT
There is a psychology to online selling—a specific way to connect with your readers—that can ensure continued sales of your front list *and* back list titles.

Here's an automated system that can be repeated daily to help you earn royalties from your growing fan base again and again.

FAITH
You're going to experience self-doubt along the way. You may even run into some naysayers who try to tell you that your books are unsaleable.

Here are words of wisdom and inspiration, from those who have succeeded before you, to help you through those times.

The Author's Money Tree: How to Grow a Bountiful Readership Organically
Amazon: https://www.amazon.com/dp/B07N41TB8N/
Kobo: https://www.kobo.com/ca/en/ebook/the-author-s-money-tree
E-Sentral: https://www.e-sentral.com/book/info/270502

The Author's Gold Rush: How to Harvest a Bountiful Crop Repeatedly
Amazon: https://www.amazon.com/dp/B07Q2Z1YXD/
Kobo: https://www.kobo.com/ca/en/ebook/the-author-s-gold-rush
E-Sentral: https://www.e-sentral.com/book/info/272881

The Author's Magic Key: How to Stay on Track and Keep the Faith
Amazon: https://www.amazon.com/gp/product/B07S1Q1H4W/
Kobo: https://www.kobo.com/ca/en/ebook/the-author-s-magic-key
E-Sentral: https://www.e-sentral.com/book/info/275408

HOW TO PRICE AN EBOOK FOR THE WESTERN WORLD VERSUS THE EASTERN WORLD

There are so many different schools of thought on how to price an ebook that it can be confusing to new independent authors. This is a passionate topic that caused quite a conflict within the publishing industry, a few years ago, as discussed in my post titled "How to Dwarf a Giant" on the PPG Publisher's Blog:

> Last year, an epic battle played out on the North American book publishing landscape.
>
> The conflict pitted an ecommerce retailer/vanity publisher against traditional trade publishers, new ideas against old, price against value, which ultimately spawned the creation of a group called Authors United led by American author Douglas Preston.
>
> In November of 2014, a soldier on the traditional side of this battle was victorious in negotiating a deal that allows trade publishers the continued right to dictate their own retail prices for the books they produce. This has always been the relationship between manufacturers and their retailers, as it should be. The manufacturer (publisher) knows its own production costs and, therefore, sets its manufacturer's suggested retail price (MSRP) based on those costs. The retailer, in turn, lists the item at that suggested price and may or may not provide discounts to their buyers based on their own projected profit margins. (Staflund, 2015)

But Amazon didn't see it this way at all, which was why the company had been playing hardball with certain trade publishers by trying to control their ebook prices on its site. It became an all-out war.

THE WAR OF THE GIANTS

The Amazon Books Team went so far as to send out a mass email to all its ebook publishers seeking support of its stance on how to price *all* ebooks *all* the time. Below is an excerpt from that email which was also published by Dave Smith for BusinessInsider.com in August of 2014:

> Just ahead of World War II, there was a radical invention that shook the foundations of book publishing. It was the paperback book. This was a time when movie tickets cost 10 or 20 cents, and books cost $2.50. The new paperback cost 25 cents – it was ten times cheaper. Readers loved the paperback and millions of copies were sold in just the first year. With it being so inexpensive and with so many more people able to afford to buy and read books, you would think the literary establishment of the day would have celebrated the invention of the paperback, yes? Nope. Instead, they dug in and circled the wagons. They believed low cost paperbacks would destroy literary culture and harm the industry (not to mention their own bank accounts). Many bookstores refused to stock them, and the early paperback publishers had to use unconventional methods of distribution – places like newsstands and drugstores....
>
> ...Well... history doesn't repeat itself, but it does rhyme.
>
> Fast forward to today, and it's the e-book's turn to be opposed by the literary establishment. Amazon and Hachette – a big US publisher and part of a $10 billion media conglomerate – are in the middle of a business dispute about e-books. We want lower e-book prices. Hachette does not. Many e-books are being released at $14.99 and even $19.99. That is unjustifiably high for an e-book. (Smith, 2014)

Is that unjustifiably high? Maybe. Maybe not. There are different schools of thought regarding how to determine the value of something that Amazon's team wasn't even willing to entertain in its argument. We're going to talk about the other side to that coin here so you have a more balanced source of information to help you determine your own prices for yourself.

VALUE-BASED MARKETING VERSUS PRICE-BASED MARKETING

Most people are already pretty comfortable with price-based marketing (e.g., offering really low prices to try to undercut one's competition) which is the form of marketing Amazon was pushing for every single ebook publisher to use on every single ebook they published. At the end of the day, *anyone* can sell based on price. But here's the biggest problem with that plan: if price is the only thing you've got, and then someone else with a similar offering comes in at a lower price than you can match, you're done. You're *finished*. You've got nowhere else to go. But if you can learn how to sell based on value, right from the start, then you'll always be able to justify your price where it is, no matter what your competition is doing. You can even increase that price, down the road, by adding more value to your overall offering.

Not everyone buys things based on price, so you should never make that assumption. Pretty much every industry has its price-based options and its value-based options: coffee (Tim Hortons versus Starbucks), food (McDonalds versus Fatburger), cars (Honda Civic versus BMW 3 Series Sedan), and the list goes on. Each of these companies caters to a different audience, and the wording one uses to speak to a price-conscious audience will be very different from the wording another will use to reach its value-conscious audience. Here are two different examples, from two different industries, intended to illustrate this point more clearly....

THE MOVING INDUSTRY

Let's say you're the director of the Records Management Department at a large corporation that has recently acquired another company. Your job is to hire a professional mover to transfer all the newly acquired confidential files from their current location to your offices downtown. You publish a Call for Tenders in your local newspaper to see what offers come in.

One offer comes in from a local moving company that positions itself as always having the best price in town. Other than that, it offers free estimates, guaranteed delivery dates, 20 years' experience, and both local and long-distance relocations for businesses and residential clients. No one at this company asks any further questions nor does any research to try to better understand a potential client's needs. They only assume everyone is after the same thing—the best price in town combined with great service—and that they'll be able to work out the details once they make the sale.

However, a second offer comes in that is more than triple the price offered by the standard moving company. This mover positions itself as a leader in the *records management* industry with over sixty years' experience in moving confidential files for all types and sizes of business clients. The primary mandate is to protect the confidentiality and integrity of every client's files. Every employee who works for this company must undergo and pass a criminal check, plus they are all put through a rigorous training program to ensure that they have a strong understanding of records management, retention, and classification schedules before they are ever allowed to touch a client's information. File moves can be managed in whatever way best suits the client (i.e., if it is important for the client to be able to access these files at all times throughout the move, this can be arranged). Finally, this mover will not only move all of the records, but it will also do a file conversion at the same time so that all of the files from the old company are labeled in the same way that files are labeled at the new company, ensuring continuity in all the information, making it easier and more efficient for employees to find it when they need it.

As the director of the Records Management Department at a large corporation who values confidentiality, efficiency, and continuity of information above all else, which of these movers would you be most likely to choose? (I don't think I have to tell you that this client went with the second, higher-priced mover.)

Sometimes price is the most important thing in the moving industry. However, sometimes value and security are more important. It all depends on the type of move being done. As with every other industry, it is crucial to understand your customer *before* you create your marketing strategy and decide on your final price.

THE EBOOK INDUSTRY

A Family for Bailey is the story of an adopted child who finds a stray dog in his back alley one evening, and who must convince his parents to adopt this animal into their home. Through this young boy's own love for the dog, it is clear to him that adoptive love is just as powerful and lasting as biological love is. Through this professionally edited, illustrated, and graphically designed storybook, both adoptive children and parents everywhere will gain insight into each other's needs and further develop their emotional attachment to each other in the process.

That's what this full colour ebook, filled with vivid imagery, is all about at its core: love and inclusion. It's not merely an ebook. It is a meaningful and tangible reminder of a family's lifelong bond—a keepsake that an adopted child can cherish for years to come.

You can't automatically slap a $2.99 USD (or lower) price onto a memento like this simply because it was published in digital format. That argument has no basis here because the *essence* of this particular ebook offers a lasting and meaningful value that extends far beyond the package it was delivered in. (Just ask the family of an adopted child who was questioning her parents' love before hearing the story, but who now trusts and knows just how cherished she is.) A price point of $14.99, and even $19.99, per ebook can *easily* be justified, in this case, with the right positioning.

It's not only about the *format*. It's about the *value* of the content within. It's about the book's target market and which marketing language—value-based marketing or price-based marketing—will best reach those buyers. It's also about the authors and publishers, themselves, and what they choose to earn from the sale of their ebooks based on their own production costs. Professionally edited, illustrated, designed, proofread, and indexed books have a much higher production cost than do-it-yourself indie books have, and their quality is noticeable better as a direct result. That commands a higher price right there, in my opinion. And that's one reason why the trade publishers fought Amazon on lowering all the ebook prices for everyone and anyone—because they have higher production costs due to the professional quality books they produce, *not* because they're evil people who want to charge consumers too much for books without good reason.

Amazon was thinking about its buyers when its Books Team wrote that open letter. But, perhaps, the company forgot about everything else—including the negative impact severely reduced prices of *everything* can have on its sellers (not to mention the overall economy) over time. There are no satisfied buyers without satisfied sellers, after all.

THREE DIFFERENT SCHOOLS OF THOUGHT

Some publishers will produce four different versions of a book, at four different price points, and release them one at a time to try to capture sales from both the value-conscious *and* price-conscious markets over time. For example, they might first release the hardcover version priced at $24.99 USD, followed by a paperback version priced at $15.99 a few months later, followed by the ebook version priced at $4.99 a few months after that, followed by the audiobook version priced at $1.99 at the very end of the launch campaign. This type of marketing tactic is more popular with the larger traditional (trade) publishers than anyone else because they have deeper pockets and can afford to produce, print, store, and distribute thousands of physical books to both online and offline markets. Not everyone can.

I do things a little differently. I personally believe it's the *content* of a book that determines its value more than the format that content is delivered in. So, for my full-length non-fiction books that have been produced as both paperbacks and ebooks, all versions are value-priced between $14.99 and $19.99 USD. However, I've also recently begun creating mini ebooks (such as the ones mentioned throughout this book) to reach all the Indie authors out there who have been trained by Amazon to buy and sell ebooks at $2.99 or lower. I've been able to charge less for those ebooks by reducing my production costs (e.g., doing much of the work, myself, rather than hiring outside help), and by splitting the full content into four mini volumes. Doing so has made it easier for me to take advantage of this "rapid release" publishing strategy and release a new ebook once every four to six weeks.

Last but not least, there are the independent authors who see it the way Amazon sees it; and they price all their books at $2.99 USD or less. In fact, many of the successful authors I've mentioned in here are using price-based marketing alone to sell their ebooks.

The moral of the story is that there are many different methods to success in this industry. I didn't add this section to try to persuade you to price your books in one way or another—only to draw your attention to the different schools of thought on how to price an ebook for the western marketplace. There are several factors to consider no matter what format of book you're publishing (and I talk about them in more detail inside this full-length publishing guide if you'd like to dive in deeper: https://polishedpublishinggroup.com/how-to-publish-a-bestselling-book/). With this information at your disposal, perhaps you'll take a closer look at the prices you chose beforehand and feel more confident in your final decision.

For more details specific to pricing ebooks for international markets, I highly recommend you read another of my recently published books titled *How to Price an Ebook: A Guide for Independent Authors*. It can be downloaded free of charge, anywhere in the world, from your choice of these three ecommerce sites:

Amazon: https://www.amazon.com/dp/B078QQ4X1Z
Kobo: https://www.kobo.com/ca/en/ebook/how-to-price-an-ebook
E-Sentral: https://www.e-sentral.com/book/info/185091

In it, I discuss how important it is for indie authors to be strategic in the way you're pricing each and every one of your ebooks. What might be considered a discount rate in one region of the world is actually considered a value-based rate in another. Your ability to understand each individual market and adjust your prices accordingly will make all the difference to your sales success around the world.

EMAIL MARKETING

I was first introduced to email marketing in late 2016 when I came across a Facebook advertisement inviting me to download a free ebook titled *The Circle of Profit: How to Turn Your Passion into an Information Business* by Anik Singal. At that time, I'd been running my own digital book publishing company for seven years; and my dream, from the start, was to successfully operate this business in a virtual office environment so I could freely travel and work with anyone, anywhere in the world, at any given time. But building this online company proved to be quite a challenge. I was still having to work elsewhere, to support myself and pay my bills, because I wasn't generating enough business to earn a decent profit. I think that's why Anik's book caught my attention—because here was this pioneer of online marketing reaching out to me through the Internet, and he was willing to share his tried and true methods regarding how to turn my passion into a successful online business once and for all.

I devoured Anik's book in full over one weekend. I even read it a second time, the following week, to ensure I fully grasped every concept and recommendation he offered. It restored my passion and renewed my hope—along with providing actual statistics and a roadmap on how to do things right. It showed me I was already on the right track in many ways, and that I should stay the course.

> Consider this: Twenty years ago if you wanted to learn something, you'd go to the library or bookstore and pick up a book. If there was new information on a topic, it had to go through a long publication process - an average of 18 months! By the time that new information came out, it was often already outdated.
>
> Today is very different.

We live in the Information Age. Basically, the greatest industry in the world today is the information industry. Those with access to information and the ability to distribute it the fastest are the ones who are poised to be our next millionaires and billionaires....

In 2012, Amazon CEO Jeff Bezos announced that Amazon's sales of digital books had surpassed their sales of physical books. Just look at how fast the Internet is growing around the world.

In the last 10 years, the number of people using the Internet has grown by 600%. It's estimated that there are more than three billion people now with access to the Internet. (Singal, 2016)

According to Anik, there were only a few things I needed to tweak to get my digital publishing business to take off once and for all; and, one of those things was to add email marketing into the mix. All these years, I'd been collecting email addresses through my blog and website. But I'd never utilized them in any way. I didn't know how. Anik was the first person to effectively explain the value of email marketing to me in a way that really resonated.

Who do you trust more: a friend or a stranger? The answer is obvious: Your friend. And when your email list subscribers start seeing you more as a friend than some random person sending them emails, you'll get the best response. (Singal, 2016)

That's what email marketing is all about. It's a powerful vehicle that allows you to reach people in a more direct and personal way than other forms of online marketing can. It is your opportunity to really engage with your readers. Become their friend by letting them know a little more about you, the person, rather than just advertising your book(s) and business to them in an impersonal way. Spend some time getting to know them a little better, too, by replying to their emailed questions with thoughtful answers.

And Anik Singal isn't the only person who swears by email marketing. In the very beginning of this book, I told you that one evening, while I was researching bestselling strategies for authors, I came across an online *Forbes* article by J. McGregor titled "Amazon Pays $450,000 A Year To This Self-Published Writer." That's when I was first introduced to a UK author named Mark Dawson who was selling massive quantities of books online, and who was more than willing to openly share his success strategies during that interview. A flame lit inside my heart when I read Mark's take on email marketing because it matched perfectly with what I'd read in Anik's book earlier. It confirmed for me that I was *definitely* on the right track.

> Dawson also credits his success to his unusual attitude towards publishing. He approaches it like a business, one in which writing is just a single cog in the media machine. He engages (responding to all fan messages) with all of his fans and focusses on building a rapport to ensure their loyalty. He holds seminars to give other writers advice and guidance. And through all of these activities, he collects names and email addresses that have amounted to a 15,000 person strong mailing list. It's through this that he disseminates his new work. What Dawson has done is essentially build a small but loyal community that translates into near guaranteed sales. (McGregor, 2015)

The readers who know and trust you will be your most responsive buyers each and every time you contact them to announce a new book, product, or service of any kind. Just ask Anik Singal and Mark Dawson. But this trust must be earned over time by providing quality, valuable content to your subscribers on a consistent basis so they stay engaged with you over the long term. Always remember there are no "quick and easy" fixes in the world of online marketing. Stay focused. Be patient with the process. Be patient with yourself. But never give up, because your efforts will be rewarded greatly if you stay the course.

On that note, I highly recommend you download and read Anik's free ebook titled *The Circle of Profit: How to Turn Your Passion into an Information Business*: http://circleofprofit.s3.amazonaws.com/The_Circle_of_Profit.pdf. It will answer every possible question you can think of regarding emailing marketing plus a few more you've probably never thought of before. By the time you're done reading it, you'll understand every who, what, where, when, why, and how that surrounds this topic.

AFFILIATE MARKETING

Another effective way to engage your fan base is to offer them incentives to help you with the promotion of your ebooks. You can offer a free copy of one or two of your books to those who are willing to share a book launch announcement with their own social media networks. Better yet, you can show your fans how to register as affiliates with the ecommerce merchant(s) you're selling your ebooks through. Once their affiliate profiles are approved by a merchant, they can then download customized affiliate links to your books that will track directly to their profiles, and they can share *those* links on their blogs and social media websites, or even via email at launch time. It's like having a 100% commission sales force working for you, no upfront investment necessary, as described in this post titled "Affiliate Marketing 101: Part I" on the Acceleration Partners® blog:

> WHAT IS AFFILIATE MARKETING?
>
> Essentially affiliate marketing involves a merchant paying a commission to other online entities, known as affiliates, for referring new business to the merchant's website. Affiliate marketing is performance-based, which means affiliates only get paid when their promotional efforts actually result in a transaction. (AccelerationPartners®, 2014)

As the author, you don't have to track or pay for anything at all. These transactions are between the affiliates and the online merchants they registered with. At the end of the day, you'll still get paid whatever royalty percentage you would normally be paid for the sale of your ebooks on each merchant's website, and the affiliate commissions will be taken care of for you in the background. It's a win-win-win scenario for you, the affiliate marketer, and the ecommerce site.

AMAZON ASSOCIATES

Amazon's affiliate program is called Amazon Associates and it can be found here: https://affiliate-program.amazon.com/home. Through this program, people can sell everything and anything Amazon has to offer—not only books. The only issue I have with their program is that affiliates must register, over and over again, for each separate website (e.g., Amazon.com, Amazon.ca, Amazon.co.uk, et cetera) in order to sell things to people around the world. That said, they've recently implemented a new strategy they call OneLink (https://affiliate-program.amazon.com/onelink/) that allows you to combine all those sites together as one after you've registered on them all. Believe me, this is a blessing. Before OneLink came along, if you included an Amazon.com affiliate link on your blog for people to purchase from, it would only work for the American buyers who made a purchase through that link. It wouldn't register as an affiliate sale for any of your other buyers outside the United States because, when *they* clicked on the link to buy the item, they would be redirected to the Amazon site in their own regions. To earn a commission from all the Amazon markets around the world, affiliates had to display separate affiliate links for every single market—and there are *several* so that was a royal pain in the butt. Luckily, OneLink has resolved that issue. Now affiliates only need to add one main Amazon.com link to their sites and the other international sales will be taken care of through it. This makes me a very happy affiliate marketer!

KOBO AFFILIATES PROGRAM

The Kobo Affiliates Program works much the same way. Although it appears their program is currently only available in six regions (e.g., Canada, US, UK, Australia, France, Germany) compared to Amazon's twelve regions (e.g., US, UK, Germany, France, Japan, Canada, China, Italy, Spain, India, Brazil, Mexico), this is a fast-growing ecommerce retailer that is quickly catching up to its competition.

I used to automatically post ebooks to both Amazon and Kobo right from the start. These days, I sometimes start off by posting a new ebook to Amazon alone so I can take advantage of the marketing programs offered exclusively to KDP Select clients (e.g., Kindle pre-orders). Once those programs have run their course, I remove the ebook from KDP Select and add it to both Kobo and E-Sentral. Selling through several merchants worldwide expands each ebook's exposure worldwide. The more exposure the better.

SOCIAL MEDIA MARKETING

Let's face it: once you get busy writing and publishing a new ebook every four to six weeks, plus engaging with your increasing client base via emailing marketing on a regular basis, you're going to have less time to spend on social media marketing. You'll still want to use it to announce new book launches, events, and other news to your followers; but, in the spirit of efficiency, it's best to focus in on only three or four sites at this time.

Which social media websites should you use? Much of that depends on the audience you're trying to reach and your own comfort level with each forum. I can personally speak to the features and benefits of Facebook, Twitter, LinkedIn, and YouTube (https://ezinearticles.com/expert/Kim_Staflund/514744) because I use them all to promote my own books on a regular basis, and they're still among the top five social media networks in the world according to eBiz MBA's recent article titled "Top 15 Most Popular Social Networking Sites | July 2017" (http://www.ebizmba.com/articles/social-networking-websites).

But there are so many more international sites to choose from as listed in Social Media Today's article titled "The World's 21 Most Important Social Media Sites and Apps in 2015" (http://www.socialmediatoday.com/social-networks/2015-04-13/worlds-21-most-important-social-media-sites-and-apps-2015) and a bab.la blog 2014 post titled "Baidu, Renren, Youku, Weibo – What are they?" (http://www.lexiophiles.com/english/baidu-renren-youku-weibo-what-are-they). The latter list of sites is definitely worth looking at for anyone interested in tapping into China's market.

I sincerely hope this book, and all the links to supplemental information and books (both free and paid) contained within, has provided you with a user-friendly roadmap toward your own success as an independent author of fiction, non-fiction, or poetry books. I hope the success stories I've shared with you have inspired you to act as much as they inspired me, and I wish you the best of success in your journey. I hope you make all your dreams come true.

That's enough chatting for now. What are you waiting for? Get started on the next ebook already! Lather, rinse, repeat!

P.S. Do you want some help with all this? If yes, then feel free to contact Polished Publishing Group (PPG) here: https://polishedpublishinggroup.com/contact-ppg/. Whatever you need help with, we've got you covered. Download our educational books. Subscribe to our blog. Enroll in our online courses. Or request a quote for our complete book publishing services.

I also recommend the following trilogy to further enhance the skills you've learned in this book. There are three necessary components to achieving your goals, no matter what those goals are: action, thought, and faith.

The Author's Holy Trinity of Profit

The Author's Money Tree	The Author's Gold Rush	The Author's Magic Key
How to Grow a Bountiful Readership Organically	How to Harvest a Bountiful Crop Repeatedly	How to Stay on Track and Keep the Faith
Kim Staflund	Kim Staflund	Kim Staflund
ACTION	**THOUGHT**	**FAITH**
Whether you self-publish or sign with a traditional publisher, you'll need a fan base (a.k.a. platform) of willing buyers to sell your books to.	There is a psychology to online selling—a specific way to connect with your readers—that can ensure continued sales of your front list *and* back list titles.	You're going to experience self-doubt along the way. You may even run into some naysayers who try to tell you that your books are unsaleable.
Here's your action plan to build that fan base—a plan that some of today's top authors are using to earn six-figure incomes.	Here's an automated system that can be repeated daily to help you earn royalties from your growing fan base again and again.	Here are words of wisdom and inspiration, from those who have succeeded before you, to help you through those times.

The Author's Money Tree: How to Grow a Bountiful Readership Organically
Amazon: https://www.amazon.com/dp/B07N41TB8N/
Kobo: https://www.kobo.com/ca/en/ebook/the-author-s-money-tree
E-Sentral: https://www.e-sentral.com/book/info/270502

The Author's Gold Rush: How to Harvest a Bountiful Crop Repeatedly
Amazon: https://www.amazon.com/dp/B07Q2Z1YXD/
Kobo: https://www.kobo.com/ca/en/ebook/the-author-s-gold-rush
E-Sentral: https://www.e-sentral.com/book/info/272881

The Author's Magic Key: How to Stay on Track and Keep the Faith
Amazon: https://www.amazon.com/gp/product/B07S1Q1H4W/
Kobo: https://www.kobo.com/ca/en/ebook/the-author-s-magic-key
E-Sentral: https://www.e-sentral.com/book/info/275408

BIBLIOGRAPHY

AccelerationPartners® (2014). *Affiliate Marketing 101: Part I.* Acceleration Partners® Blog. Retrieved July 22, 2019, from http://www.accelerationpartners.com/blog/affiliate-marketing-101-part-i.

Alter, A. (2016, March 21). *James Patterson Has a Big Plan for Small Books.* Retrieved July 24, 2019, from The New York Times: https://www.nytimes.com/2016/03/22/business/media/james-patterson-has-a-big-plan-for-small-books.html.

Biddulph, R. (2017, July). *A Non-Fiction Self-Published Author Success Story with Ryan Biddulph.* Retrieved July 21, 2019, from PPG Publisher's Blog: http://blog.polishedpublishinggroup.com/2017/06/a-non-fiction-self-published-author-success-story-with-ryan-biddulph/.

Bowker. (2014). *FAQs: General Questions.* Retrieved July 24, 2019, from ISBN.org by Bowker: http://www.isbn.org/faqs_general_questions#isbn_faq1.

Chesson, D. (2017, July). *How to Unlock the Secret Kindle Categories.* Retrieved July 24, 2019, from Kindlepreneur: https://kindlepreneur.com/how-to-unlock-the-secret-kindle-categories/.

Clarke, A. (2019). In *SEO 2019: Learn Search Engine Optimization With Smart Internet Marketing Strategies. [Kindle version].* United States: Simple Effectiveness Publishing. Available from Amazon.

Dawson, M. (2016). *SPF-013: How to Launch a Book: A Detailed Look at Mark Dawson's Recent Book Launch.* Retrieved July 19, 2019, from The Self Publishing Formula Podcast:

http://selfpublishingformula.libsyn.com/spf-013-how-to-launch-a-book-a-detailed-look-at-mark-dawsons-recent-book-launch.

Foster, J. D. (2017, July). *The Ins and Out of Outlines: Plotters Versus Pansters [PART I: PLOTTERS]*. Retrieved July 22, 2019, from PPG Publisher's Blog: http://blog.polishedpublishinggroup.com/2017/06/the-ins-and-out-of-outlines-plotters-versus-pansters-part-i-plotters/.

Haden, J. (2018, May 21). *The Motivation Myth. How High Achievers Really Set Themselves Up To Win with Jeff Haden*. Retrieved July 22, 2019, from The Creative Penn: https://www.thecreativepenn.com/2018/05/21/the-motivation-myth-how-high-achievers-really-set-themselves-up-to-win-with-jeff-haden/.

Massenzio, D. (2015). *The Importance of an Editor and Beta Readers for Independent Authors*. Don Massenzio's Blog. Retrieved July 19, 2019, from https://donmassenzio.wordpress.com/2015/02/14/the-importance-of-an-editor-and-beta-readers-for-independent-authors/.

McGregor, J. (2015, April 15). Amazon Pays $450,000 A Year To This Self-Published Writer. *Forbes.com.* Retrieved July 20, 2019, from https://www.forbes.com/sites/jaymcgregor/2015/04/17/mark-dawson-made-750000-from-self-published-amazon-books/#7253e38a6b5b.

Penn 1, J. (2014, October 14). *Six Figure Success Self-Publishing Non-Fiction Books With Steve Scott*. Retrieved July 22, 2019, from The Creative Penn: https://www.thecreativepenn.com/2014/10/14/non-fiction-success/.

Penn 2, J. (2017, March). *How To Self-Publish An Ebook*. Retrieved July 22, 2019, from The Creative Penn: https://www.thecreativepenn.com/how-to-self-publish-an-ebook/.

Pilkington, E. (2012, January 12). *Amanda Hocking, the writer who made millions by self-publishing online*. Retrieved July 22, 2019, from The Guardian: https://www.theguardian.com/books/2012/jan/12/amanda-hocking-self-publishing.

Provost, G. (2017). *100 Ways to Improve Your Writing: Proven Professional Techniques for Writing with Style and Power*. Published October 1st 1985 by Berkley.

Rose, J. (2019, July 17). *Passive Income Ideas You Can Start Today*. Retrieved July 22, 2019, from Good Financial Cents: https://www.goodfinancialcents.com/passive-income-ideas/.

Sansevieri, P. (2013, July). *Keys to Understanding Amazon's Algorithms*. The Book Designer: Practical Advice to Help Build Better Books. Retrieved July 24, 2019 from https://www.thebookdesigner.com/2013/07/amazon-algorithms/.

Shofner, A. (2019, February 26). *6 Automatic Editing Tools That Will Make Your Writing Super Clean*. Retrieved July 22, 2019, from The Write Life: http://thewritelife.com/automatic-editing-tools/.

Singal, A. (2016). *The Circle of Profit: How to Turn Your Passion into an Information Business FREE EBOOK*. Retrieved July 21, 2019, from http://circleofprofit.s3.amazonaws.com/The_Circle_of_Profit.pdf.

Smith, D. (2014). *AMAZON: 'Email Hachette And Copy Us'*. BusinessInsider.com. Retrieved January 1, 2018, from http://www.businessinsider.com/amazon-is-emailing-authors-to-go-after-hachette--heres-their-message-2014-8.

Staflund, K. (2014). *How to Publish a Bestselling Book ... and Sell It WORLDWIDE Based on Value, Not Price!* Canada: Polished Publishing Group.

Staflund, K. (2015, November). *How to Dwarf a Giant*. PPG Publisher's Blog. Retrieved July 23, 2019, from https://blog.polishedpublishinggroup.com/2015/11/how-to-dwarf-a-giant/.

Staflund, K. (2017). *Profitable Publishing Today: Start Earning Money as an Author Without Quitting Your Day Job*. [Kindle version]. Canada: Polished Publishing Group. Available from Amazon.

Stone, M. (2017). *TCK Publishing*. Should You Turn Your Book Into an Audiobook on Audible? Retrieved July 22, 2019, from: https://www.tckpublishing.com/should-you-turn-your-book-into-an-audiobook-on-audible/.

INDEX

ADDITIONAL RESOURCES

IMPORTANT ADVICE REGARDING AMAZON AUTHOR CENTRAL PAGES

LinkedIn Pulse Article | 3 Ways an Author Central Page Can Spike Your Ranking on Amazon: https://www.linkedin.com/pulse/3-ways-author-central-page-can-spike-your-ranking-amazon-kim-staflund.

FREE BOOKS ON PUBLISHING

Download any of these FREE BOOKS from your choice of Amazon, Kobo, or E-Sentral. Inside, you'll learn important tips on how to navigate this mysterious book publishing business littered with acronyms and peculiar old-fashioned practices: https://polishedpublishinggroup.com/free-books/.

ADDITIONAL HELPFUL BOOKS

Successful Selling Tips for Introverted Authors (.EPUB and .MOBI Ebooks, Paperback)

- Kobo .EPUB: https://www.kobo.com/ca/en/ebook/successful-selling-tips-for-introverted-authors-1
- Amazon .MOBI: https://www.amazon.com/dp/B06XQK4ZDW
- E-Sentral .EPUB: https://www.e-sentral.com/book/info/183102
- Order in the paperback from any local bookstore such as Barnes and Nobel: https://www.barnesandnoble.com/w/successful-selling-tips-for-introverted-authors-kim-staflund/1122780400

- Read the reviews here:
  https://polishedpublishinggroup.com/successful-selling-tips-for-introverted-authors/

How to Publish a Bestselling Book ... and Sell It WORLDWIDE Based on Value, Not Price! (.EPUB and .MOBI Ebooks, Paperback)

- Kobo .EPUB:
  https://www.kobo.com/ca/en/ebook/how-to-publish-a-bestselling-book-and-sell-it-worldwide-based-on-value-not-price
- Amazon .MOBI:
  https://www.amazon.com/dp/B06XQK7X7S
- E-Sentral .EPUB:
  https://www.e-sentral.com/book/info/183099
- Order in the paperback from any local bookstore such as Barnes and Nobel:
  https://www.barnesandnoble.com/w/how-to-publish-a-bestselling-book-and-sell-it-worldwide-based-on-value-not-price-kim-staflund/1120044163
- Read the reviews here:
  https://polishedpublishinggroup.com/how-to-publish-a-bestselling-book/

How to Publish a Book in Canada ... and Sell Enough Copies to Make a Profit! (.EPUB and .MOBI Ebooks, Paperback)

- Kobo .EPUB:
  https://www.kobo.com/ca/en/ebook/how-to-publish-a-book-in-canada-and-sell-enough-copies-to-make-a-profit-1
- Amazon .MOBI:
  https://www.amazon.com/dp/B00GVGG1BE
- Order in the paperback from any local bookstore such as Barnes and Nobel:
  https://www.barnesandnoble.com/w/how-to-publish-a-book-in-canada-and-sell-enough-copies-to-make-a-profit-kim-staflund/1117050612

- Read the reviews here: https://polishedpublishinggroup.com/how-to-publish-a-book-in-canada/

ONLINE COURSES FOR AUTHORS [LEARN FROM HOME]

Bookmark this page and visit it often to view the latest recommended online courses for authors: https://polishedpublishinggroup.com/online-courses-for-authors/. Many more affordable courses are coming soon to PPG. Here is where you can:

- enhance your writing skills;
- uncover effective book sales and marketing techniques;
- master audiobook production;
- perfect your ebook creation and conversion abilities;
- learn how to best utilize Microsoft Office;
- and even study professional graphic design with an Adobe-certified instructor.

ABOUT THE AUTHOR

So many people are publishing books of all kinds nowadays, and they need guidance regarding best practices with everything from writing to publishing to selling those books. I've made it my life's mission to help others navigate this mysterious business littered with acronyms and peculiar old-fashioned practices.

As a bestselling author and TESOL certified sales coach for authors with over 25 years' experience in the North American English book publishing industry (in both the traditional and contemporary markets), I can show you how to write, publish, advertise, sell, market, and publicize your book(s) using all the effective traditional and online tricks of the trade. Add my substantial advertising sales and marketing background into the mix, and you have a serious mentor in front of you who can help you achieve commercial success as an author in the traditional "bricks and mortar" bookstores as well as online.

Visit my website and blog here:
https://www.polishedpublishinggroup.com/